h
6.07

Listening to Young People in School,
Youth Work and Counselling

also by Nick Luxmoore

Working with Anger and Young People
ISBN 1 84310 466 0

of related interest

Supporting Parents of Teenagers
A Handbook for Professionals
Edited by John Coleman and Debi Roker
ISBN 1 85302 944 0

Dream Time with Children
Learning to Dream, Dreaming to Learn
Brenda Mallon
ISBN 1 84310 014 2

How We Feel
An Insight into the Emotional World of Teenagers
Edited by Jacki Gordon and Gillian Grant
ISBN 1 85302 439 2

Understanding Drugs
A Handbook for Parents, Teachers and Other Professionals
David Emmett and Graeme Nice
ISBN 1 85302 400 7

Troubles of Children and Adolescents
Edited by Ved Varma
ISBN 1 85302 323 X

Group Work with Children and Adolescents
A Handbook
Edited by Dr Kedar Nath Dwivedi
ISBN 1 85302 157 1

Active Analytic Group Therapy for Adolescents
John Evans
ISBN 1 85302 616 6

Contemporary Art Therapy with Adolescents
Shirley Riley
ISBN 1 85302 637 9

Listening to Young People in School, Youth Work and Counselling

Nick Luxmoore

Jessica Kingsley Publishers
London and Philadelphia

First published in the United Kingdom in 2000 by
Jessica Kingsley Publishers
116 Pentonville Road
London N1 9JB, UK
and
400 Market Street, Suite 400
Philadelphia, PA 19106, USA

www.jkp.com

Library of Congress Cataloging in Publication Data
Luxmoore, Nick, 1956–
    Listening to young people in school, youth work and counselling / Nick
    Luxmoore.
    p. cm.
    Includes bibliographical references (p.) and index.
    ISBN 1-85302-909-2 (pbk. : alk. paper)
    1. Educational counseling--Great Britain. 2. Youth--Counseling of--Great
    Britain. I. Title.
    LB1027.5.L86 2000
    373.14--dc21   00-041265

British Library Cataloguing in Publication Data
A CIP catalogue record for this book is available from the British Library

ISBN-13: 978 1 85302 909 7
ISBN-10: 1 85302 909 2

Printed and Bound in Great Britain by
Athenaeum Press, Gateshead, Tyne and Wear

Contents

For Kathy, Frances and Julia

Acknowledgements

This book was originally written as a series of occasional articles for friends and colleagues. My idea was to explore the overlaps between various ways of working with and thinking about young people. Until recently I managed a counselling and information service for young people and worked as a secondary school counsellor. I used to be a teacher and used to run a youth centre.

Versions of some of the chapters have been published variously by the British Psychodrama Association, the Oxford Psychotherapy Society, Oxfordshire County Council and the *Peer Support Networker* (Roehampton Institute, London).

I'm grateful to the many people whose ideas and experience have informed my thinking and whose trust and support have allowed me to do my work.

I'm also grateful to Penguin UK and to Alfred A. Knopf, a division of Random House Inc. for permission to quote from Albert Camus' *The Outsider*; to Methuen Publishing Ltd. for permission to quote from Edward Bond's play, *The Sea*; to PBJ Management for permission to quote from *Harry Enfield and Chums*; to Windswept Music (London) Ltd for permission to quote from Joni Mitchell's song, 'All I want'; to International Music Publications for permission to quote from Sandy Denny's song, 'What is true?' © Jardiniere Music/Intersong Music Ltd., from The Doors' song, 'People are strange', © Nipper Music Co. Inc./Doors Music Co, USA, and from Supergrass' song, 'Alright', words and music by Daniel Goffey, Gareth Coombes and Michael Quinn © 1995 EMI Music Publishing Ltd. London WC2H 0EA, reproduced by permission of International Music Publications Ltd. I'm grateful to The Society of Authors as the literary representative of the estate of A.E. Housman for permission to quote two lines from 'poem XII, Last Poems' from *The Collected Poems of A.E. Housman*, ©1922 by Henry Holt and Co., © 1950 by Barclays Bank Ltd. My best attempts to contact J. Patrick Lewis for permission to quote from his poem, 'New Baby', have so far failed. If anyone can let me know of the author's correct whereabouts I will rectify this.

CHAPTER I

Kevin

In Defence of Thirteen-year-old Boys

His birthday presents await him. Kevin sits excitedly with his Mum and Dad: a charming twelve-year-old boy, waiting for the clock to strike midnight and his thirteenth birthday to begin.

The clock strikes but, to his parents' complete astonishment, their charming son explodes into Kevin the teenager, a thirteen-year-old with a vengeance. 'I hate you! You're always blaming me! It's so unfair! Can't you see you're ruining my life?' Mum and Dad sit dumbstruck as Kevin the teenager stomps off into a self-inflicted future (Harry Enfield 1997).

We laugh because we recognise. We've been like Kevin and, looking back, teenage behaviour does seem funny: funny because it's so unnecessary. Kevin seems such a fool: so clumsy, inarticulate, selfish, so *ugly*.

Thirteen-year-old boys, the men and fathers of the future, often *do* seem like this. They *are* unattractive. Other chapters in the book will explore some of the difficulties experienced by girls but, compared to boys, girls can appear altogether more grown-up and sensible. Boys can be rude, smelly, thoughtless, antisocial, cruel, sexist, racist: everything that might make us want to consign them to the depths. He's unreachable, we say. He won't be helped. He'll just have to learn the hard way. Ah well, it's his loss …

Boys have mixed feelings about this reaction. It absolutely delights them but at the same time they despair of it. And we carry on hating them for what they've become. We ignore, blame, and in some vague way, want to see them punished.

Slowly, but surely, we abandon them.

I think this is unfair. Part of my job, working for a young people's counselling and information service, involved going into schools to work with groups of students where, for one reason or another, the prevailing culture in the group was preventing them from learning effectively. At one point I was working with two groups of Year 8 boys (12- to 13-year-olds) in different schools. They had various things in common.

In both schools they were advertised to me as 'the worst class in the school', so I expected a couple of dozen small sadists, intent upon my destruction. Instead I found two groups of extremely enthusiastic thirteen-year-old boys. True, they found it hard to listen to one another for any length of time. In other words, they *talked* an awful lot and this may have been what made them 'the worst class in the school', but in both cases their talk was out of sheer enthusiasm.

They were anxious, they had important things to say and they thought their thirteen-year-old jokes were very funny. My dilemma, running the groups, was how to keep their enthusiasm while focusing them on the group's task which was all about listening to one another, exploring feelings and attitudes, developing self-esteem and confidence. In the first sessions I was irritated by so much talking and felt myself wanting to be publicly cross, using my authority to shut them up. But I knew that to do so would be to scare them and make it harder for them to trust me. They seemed genuinely affectionate towards one another, though a thirteen-year-old boy's dilemma is how on earth to show that. Sometimes a punch on the shoulder can be a way of trying to say, 'I like you.'

What emerged from both groups was that they *already* felt that people were against them; that the girls in the class were favoured; that they themselves were regarded as uninterested in work, as unruly, lazy, destructive. My guess is that their constant talking resulted in teachers seeming angry with *them*, rather than with their talking. Both groups were indignant and clearly upset by what they felt was a misrepresentation. They heard people saying they were stupid. Curiously, it also emerged that both groups of boys had felt closely attached to their male form tutors the year before, in Year 7, when they were eleven to twelve years old. At the end of that year, for various practical reasons, they were allocated new form tutors with whom they were now struggling. It seemed that the way these changes had been handled by the schools had left the boys feeling hurt.

Probably, the schools had underestimated the nature and strength of the boys' attachment to their first form tutors. Schools tend to do these things in an administrative rush, assuming that such changes don't really matter (this is Big School, after all!), but perhaps also, crucially, assuming that big boys don't notice, don't make important attachments: big boys can get over anything. Here, it seemed, two groups of boys, feeling taken for granted, feeling hurt, would be taking their particular revenge on their schools for some time to come.

Culturally, we're worried by boys. Shakespeare refers casually to boys being 'wanton' in *King Lear*, and for years *Lord of the Flies* (Golding 1954) has stood as a sort of explication of *how boys are*. There has been no female equivalent. This hasn't been seen as a novel about humans descending into chaos. This has been seen as being about *boys*. Set for public examinations year after year, it's become almost a national cautionary tale. And more recently James Bulger's murder has again stamped on our consciousness the awful, apparently callous, cruelty of boys. We recoil.

Blake Morrison's (1997) account of the Bulger trial searches throughout for answers to the question, why did Robert Thompson and Jon Venables kill James Bulger? At the trial no answers were forthcoming and Morrison finds none in the surrounding detail. The boys knew right from wrong, it was said, but they still killed James. So the question haunts us. Boys stand accused and become more frightening because we can't understand. There simply remains our suspicion that, as Robert

Thompson told his psychiatrist before the trial, 'All little boys are nice until they get older' (p.95).

In the remake of *Tombstone* (Jacks, Daniel, Misiorowski, Vajna 1993) Wyatt Earp and Doc Holliday discuss Ringo, the chief baddie, who just won't stop being bad. Earp asks Doc what he thinks Ringo really wants in life. The Doc replies that he thinks Ringo acts the way he does because he wants revenge – for having been born. Whether or not this serves as adequate psychological insight into Ringo, it does suggest that men do bad things because they are essentially angry and, perhaps beneath their anger, hurt: perhaps from birth and childhood, perhaps because later (as thirteen-year-olds?) they discover that no one really likes them. It's well documented that suicide among boys and young men is increasing alarmingly but, interestingly, it's suggested that, rather than being an expression of hopeless sadness, suicide might sometimes be a way of protecting other people from anger. *I feel so angry I could kill someone.* Boys are often trapped in anger, unable to express hurt feelings any other way. Girls can be just as trapped, but in tears and crying.

On his deathbed Doc Holliday, the hard-living rogue, incapable of taking responsibility, appraises Wyatt Earp, his opposite, the stubborn law-enforcer eschewing pleasure for principle. How, we've been wondering, have these two opposites become friends? Doc explains why he was drawn to Earp, saying with his last words that he was the only person ever to give him hope.

I think this is important. Doc is attached to Earp because Earp provides boundaries, enforces rules, and without rules Doc knows he himself can't function and towns like Tombstone will forever be prey to marauding bands of bad men. Perhaps one of the reasons thirteen-year-old boys are sometimes so attracted to fascist leaders and fascist solutions to problems is because of the boys' own need for clarity, simplicity, rules. Compassion and forgiveness are too slippery. Boys desperately need to experience them but at the same time they need to feel safe and contained. Wyatt

Earp becomes a sort of father-figure for Tombstone: humane but also a stickler for principle, holding the town together while also letting it breathe, as a father might hold a son. Earp doesn't despise the townspeople. He accepts them, accepts his responsibility to help them and, like boys, they begin to learn.

Like many American heroes Wyatt Earp and Doc Holliday come as a pair. We might think of Tom Sawyer and Huck Finn, Butch and Sundance, Starsky and Hutch, countless others (Fiedler 1960). There are exceptions, but in the UK our heroic tradition is more of the solitary male without a buddy at his side. Perhaps this is a homophobic tradition. Perhaps it's that lots of boys and men don't know how to be comfortably intimate with other males – and if this is the case, then the roots of this discomfort must lie in our relationships with our fathers, our first potential buddies.

In my experience many boys have very diminished relationships with their fathers. They have no idea what makes them tick. All they know is an uncommunicative man, full of feeling but utterly at a loss as to how to express it appropriately. Sometimes the man is violent, sometimes sarcastic, sometimes simply absent. One question I often ask boys, whether in groups or in individual counselling, is 'What sort of a father would you aim to be?' The answer comes straight back, often from boys whose only experience has been of fathers like those I've just described: 'I'd always be there for my kids. I'd listen to them. I'd stick up for them. I'd do things with them. I'd be strict but not too strict.' The boys have clearly got this vision from somewhere, and it's hard to believe they've got it from their own fathers if their fathers really are as they're described. Perhaps the vision has come from films or other adults.

Certainly teachers, youth workers and others must have a crucial role to play in this regard, amending boys' experience of fathering. The role involves kindness and care but it also involves setting and adhering to boundaries: rules without which no one can feel safe. Boys (and girls) will argue with rules

('I hate you!' says Kevin. 'It's so unfair!'), but they need adults not to be scared of having rules and not to be scared of having arguments about rules. Without adult leadership boys create their own leaders, often disastrously.

I used to be based in a youth centre where each week we ran a deliberately structured evening for boys. The first part of the evening was a chance to hang out and relax, at the end of which there was a curfew after which no one new could join us. People could leave, but they weren't allowed back. Then for about 45 minutes we ran a compulsory session, meticulously thought out each week according to what my co-worker and I thought the boys needed. Sometimes we focused on sex, sometimes families, sometimes self-esteem, sometimes on other issues. Our belief was that you rarely change people's attitudes merely by challenging them verbally. People will only open themselves to new ideas if they're feeling safe and feeling valued themselves.

Each session was extremely tightly organised, almost always using some form of game structure as 'the point' of what we were doing but always using serious content. The final part of the evening was football in the sports hall: the crucial carrot which kept the boys with us for the whole evening. Officially, football was why they bothered to come at all. Unofficially, secretly, we knew they valued the structured work, but it was only made possible for them because it was compulsory, protected by a curfew and with football as a final reward. They would complain, 'This is so boring!', but they knew complaining would make no difference.

I remember when I worked as a teacher how annoying it was to be met with the refrain, 'This is so boring!' Sometimes it *was* boring, they were right, I was giving them work for work's sake. But sometimes it wasn't boring at all and that was frustrating. I think then the refrain translated as 'I don't understand this and I don't understand why it matters.'

This is important. Teenagers are philosophical. They want to know why things are the way they are; what the purpose or meaning is. This includes: why do we live? why do we bother to do anything? Important questions. Without answers it's hard to place oneself in the world, to prioritise things, to give a damn. And in their frustration, their busyness or their fear, adults don't always answer satisfactorily. In school the Big Answer is exams – *that's* why we do things – which every philosophical teenager knows isn't a good enough answer. So other answers are trotted out: jobs, families, money, God. Rarely do we allow or encourage teenagers just to think about meaninglessness, maybe for fear that they'll lapse into apathy or depression but maybe also because of our own fear of death and meaning-lessness. If we've spent our lives creating distractions so as not to think about these things, then a philosophical teenager disturbs it all. So the question is slapped down, the questioner made to feel like a time-waster.

I think that not having big answers to offer oneself is reas-suring rather than frightening for teenagers. It means that the question was a good one, the questioner right to be asking, and the adult is respectful enough of the teenager to be honest about also wondering. Why *do* we exist? Why *do* we do things? Some of what we despise in teenage boys' behaviour might really be their roundabout way of asking, 'What's the point?' We need to pick up on the question, applaud it and start talking about it. Nietzsche said, 'If we possess our *why* of life we can put up with almost any *how*' (trans. Hollingdale 1968, p.33). Until they have some whys teenagers (boys *and* girls) naturally resent and attack every single how. And cheap and easy whys, tripping compla-cently off adult tongues, just seem contemptible.

It's much easier to say why not and what we are not. When we convene for a first session, the groups I run for teenage boys in schools are charged with anxiety. The boys want to be there because of secretly wanting to talk, but at the same time they dread being there for fear of exposure. So they sit, waiting for me to start, teasing each other and play-fighting. To begin with they put all their faith in me, like children, unable to trust themselves or each other. To say anything about themselves is far too embarrassing, so one of the first things we do is to go round the group several times with each person saying, 'One thing I'm *not* is …' There can be no repetition. Someone will say, 'One thing I'm not is gay', and someone else, 'One thing I'm not is a girl.' The exercise actually allows the group to voice its anxieties. 'One thing I'm not is stupid. One thing I'm not is good at sport.' Once these things have been said the group seems to relax and we can move on to the harder 'One thing I *am* is …' and 'One thing I'd *like to be* is …' without so much embarrassment getting in the way.

These groups are particularly anxious about sexuality and therefore about touch. When they first sit down there's much jockeying for position – 'Sit by me! I've kept this seat for you!' Simply sitting next to people is uncomfortable, so we do exercises where, by virtue of the rules, everyone has to swap seats. This then makes it permissible to sit next to comparative strangers, for it's impossible to talk meaningfully until this physical, sexual anxiety has been dealt with. A favourite exercise is one where a team of boys lies side by side on their fronts, facing the same direction, shoulder to shoulder. The other team lies opposite. On the command 'Go!' the boy furthest away rolls over all his team-mates and comes to a halt beyond the last boy. As soon as the second boy has been rolled over, he in turn begins rolling, followed by the third boy and so on. The winning team is the one which, caterpillar-like, reaches the end of the room first. This involves intense physical contact, body to body, but the boys allow themselves to be distracted by the thought of winning and so free themselves to enjoy it. No one suggests that this is a 'gay' thing to do. Afterwards we begin to talk, having got the physical stuff out of the way.

In the same way I remember supervising outdoor swimming sessions at the youth centre. Each summer we would buy a large dinghy and on Wednesday evenings the blown-up dinghy would be thrown into the pool. The boys would then spend the *whole* of their allocated hour in the pool each week attacking and pummelling the dinghy, climbing into it, getting tipped out, tipping other people out, climbing back in. It was good fun and exhaustingly physical, body to body, flesh to flesh throughout, but amongst the cross-section of relatively homophobic boys, nobody ever said, 'Eugh, this is gay!' It was as if everyone knew that to say that would ruin everything and they'd no longer be able to continue their fun. Just one comment would have made everyone self-conscious. I think their actual hunger for and enjoyment of physical touch was so great that this unspoken conspiracy pertained when, in any other context, the boys would have poured scorn on one another for even accidentally touching another boy.

Because boys can seem so inconsistent, relishing this week what they despised last week, I find myself, in supervising counsellors who work with young people, coming back again and again to the idea of ambivalence. It's true of adults as well, but certainly true that teenagers rarely experience a straightforward feeling. Close to 'I hate you!' will be 'I love you!' Beneath 'I'm angry!' will be 'I'm afraid' or 'I'm hurt.' 'I wish you'd go away!' will often mask 'I wish we could be closer.' Teenagers feel *both* feelings at the same time, usually pulling in different directions.

That's what ambivalence is. 'I want to be independent/dependent. I don't care what people think of me/I care desperately.' Behind the cynic is the idealist waiting to come out. Behr (1988) writes about teasing as *ambivalent* communication in groups of young people, setting up intimacy while simultaneously pushing someone further away. Teasing, he writes, is a way of avoiding painful feelings. It might be argued that the journey from adolescence to adulthood is all about learning to manage ambivalent feelings. Teenagers flip back and forth: hostile one minute, loving the next. Adults have usually learnt to steer a steadier course.

Thirteen-year-old boys tease one another constantly because they feel ambivalent constantly. The physical pile-ups I've already described (rolling over one another and playing with the dinghy) will sometimes become violent. Someone will have held on to someone else just too long or pushed too hard. Then suddenly one boy will lash out at another and swift intervention is necessary. It reminds me of Klein's (1932) thinking about child development: the way the happy, suckling baby will one day suddenly bite the mother's nipple. At once ambivalence is born. The breast is no longer straightforwardly nurturing but becomes also a focus of frustration and anger. By extension, thirteen-year-old boys long for comfort and love, physical tenderness, but also rage against anything resembling those things. Because those things are so lovely, it hurts to be separated from them. Hence beneath the anger, the hurt.

Harry Enfield has another character, a boy of about two called Harry who perpetually bullies his year-old sister, Lulu. We laugh again at the recognisable arbitrariness of Harry's cruelty. *That's just what little boys are like.* He pushes Lulu over, then immediately pleads innocence to his accusing mother. Only in a later episode do we get some insight into Harry's behaviour where he coaxes Lulu into a large wooden chest, shuts the lid, sits on it and, when their mother comes in wondering where Lulu is, says, 'Lulu gone back to heaven!' Triumphantly, Harry reaches his adoring arms towards his mother.

But there's no going back to the way things were, so children like Harry attach themselves to transitional objects (Winnicott 1971), essentially substitutes upon which to heap their attention, enthusiasm, affection. Small boys may have bits of rag to suck, teddy bears to cling to. A thirteen-year-old boy may be attached to many transitional objects: a computer, a football team, a new bike, trainers. Drugs might also be thought of as transitional objects: at one extreme replacing mother with another completely dependent relationship and at another simply providing some low-key stimulation or comfort.

Sometimes the enthusiasms of thirteen-year-old boys seem narrow, pointless, silly, but I think it's important to wonder about the *emotional meaning* of these objects. A computer might be about discovering some control, finding order in things. A favourite football team might be about belonging to a different kind of family, becoming a man, dealing with success and failure. It's often said that Nick Hornby's (1992, 1995) first two books were responsible for the rise of New Laddism: that 1990s mix of comedy, sex and beer masquerading as wit and intelligence in men. I think this misses the point. In both cases the subjects of the novels (Arsenal football club and record-collecting) are transitional objects from which Hornby's alter egos can't move on. The characters acknowledge and bemoan this fact. They're stuck. Relationships with real people are far harder than with a football team or a record collection. The same process applies to thirteen-year-old boys. They too get stuck, for a while, with their many transitional objects, until they're ready to move on to the complexities of real people and real relationships. There's nothing silly about this. Even as adults we maintain particular enthusiasms in modified forms. Where would we be without our cars, houses, digital gadgets: the many objects of our affections?

To some extent the teacher and youth worker also serve as transitional objects, adored or reviled. More accurately, they represent transitional relationships in a boy's (or girl's) life. Because the process of separating from mother and father, becoming 'individual', is such an anxious one, boys attach themselves instead to other adults. I remember a perennial problem at the youth centre was how to help boys move on from a child–parent relationship with the centre itself. Some would gradually stop using the centre anyway; others I would be able to involve in more sophisticated projects (bands, plays), and others would move on to taking more responsibility for the running of the centre as workers themselves. But most years there would be a particular group, and they would always be boys, who would get stuck. Unless I found a way of helping them through this transition we would eventually end up having a row. They would stubbornly force the issue about some rule, leaving me no choice but to ban them from the centre. They would then gleefully storm off, swearing, wishing me and the centre dead. And they would never come back. The row had served its purpose, pushing them on from their stuck position. I would see them around and they'd be friendly, asking how things were going, as if their row with me had never happened. They were free.

This happens, of course, in families and it happens with girls as well as boys, but at the youth centre the girls had always already moved on, embracing more responsible roles or long since having left to spend time with their older boyfriends. This was part of what was difficult for the boys. Every thirteen-year-old boy knows that girls develop physically ahead of boys. This is *galling* and terribly unfair on boys. A thirteen-year-old girl treats a thirteen-year-old boy as a subspecies from the planet Child. Thirteen-year-old girls are usually interested in much older boys so younger boys are left bemused, desperate to catch up physically and anxious to make amends for their evident uselessness. Hostility is one convenient defence against feeling useless. Boys will attack in other boys the very things they find uncomfortable in themselves. Feeling despised, they'll make themselves despicable.

And then sometimes they'll fight. There seems to be a delicate connection between the two things boys exaggerate about most, fighting and sex, where 'I could *have* you!' somehow suggests both a violent and a sexual intention. Perhaps fighting expresses for boys something sexual that can't otherwise find expression. It's important not to underestimate the degree of anxiety boys feel about sexuality and sex. They talk about it a lot, usually through jokes, but nothing seems to take away the misery. Harry Enfield's Kevin is reduced to speechless jelly whenever a girl appears. His attempts to look cool merely make him look stupid until in one episode by some fluke the grumbling, monosyllabic teenager gets lucky, disappearing upstairs with a girl at a party. He emerges, some time later, grinning ecstatically, and the next morning at breakfast his long-suffering parents find that their long-lost, charming son Kevin has suddenly returned, polite and helpful as he was before his thirteenth birthday. They have no idea why this has happened but we, the audience, know why. *It* happened and, for Kevin, one massive teenage anxiety has disappeared.

It hurts to feel unwanted. Wherever they look, Kevin and other thirteen-year-old boys are surrounded by negative images of themselves. Men throughout the world are charged with its worst horrors and so thirteen-year-old boys find it much easier to describe their *worst* features than their best. Surrounded by so much self-doubt and cynicism about men, some are only too happy to adopt a yuppie philosophy: I'm all that matters; if I gain at other people's expense then that's their lookout; it's not my problem. Instantly we rail against this, call them antisocial and tell them that they should *take* responsibility. Freedom, we say, comes only with responsibility, yet the kind of responsibility we suggest boys take is for things like tidying their bedrooms, doing their homework, thinking about their appearance. Rarely do we offer them responsibility for other people.

This may be partly because we're scared to do so (the image of the two boys leading James Bulger away haunts everyone), but partly because we simply don't create enough opportunities in the first place. Where there *are* a few opportunities, girls have already taken them. In the youth centre there would be an overall youth committee, a gig committee, an arts festival com-mittee and so on. Most committee members would be girls. Where there were opportunities for people to help run junior discos, almost all the helpers would be girls. Yet where a boy *would* volunteer to help he would almost invariably be a success: conscientious, hard-working and kind.

In schools where I support teams of Year 13 students (17- to 18-year-olds) who work with younger students girls again dominate but yet again, where a boy does volunteer, he almost always turns out to be very successful and I have to remember this at interviews. After several articulate, sincere girls well able to describe their feelings and reasons for wanting to do the job have been interviewed, a single boy will stumble into the interview room. He may sit uncomfortably, may not make much eye contact, may give very short answers. I have to remember I'm not selecting student counsellors for their abilities at interview. If I were, there would be no male student counsellors at all. I have to remember that boys *can* take responsibility, that underneath the awkwardness are compassion and real anger about the world's injustices. This is true of younger boys as well. We don't create opportunities for them. Carefully prepared and monitored thirteen-year-old boys helping in specific ways in primary schools is not unimaginable. Similarly supported older boys running small discussion groups in school for younger boys about bullying, sex, families and so on ought not to be impossible.

We ask boys who are in trouble to explain what happened and why they did it. They can answer the first bit but usually not the second. The why part is too complicated. It's up to *adults* to think about and understand why.

Speaking after the murder of James Bulger, John Major said, 'We must condemn a little more and understand a little less.' I think that, on the contrary, we need to understand much more but perhaps the most important thing we can do is to *like* thirteen-year-old boys. Compassion seems a more useful starting point than condemnation.

CHAPTER 2

Siblings

The Possibility of Therapeutic Relationships between Young People

However reluctantly, we'll admit to being the product of parents. In fact, we take considerable account of relationships with mothers and fathers but traditionally pay less attention to those other members of the family from whom we also derive an identity: our siblings.

Part of my work in schools has involved helping set up, train and supervise teams of older students (usually called student counsellors or listeners) whose job for a year is to get to know as many younger students as possible and be available to them as a source of support throughout the year. The student counsellors do this in a variety of ways. But while it's easy to describe what their work practically consists of, it's harder to explain exactly what goes on in these relationships and why they're usually so treasured by both the student counsellors and the younger students. Something important clearly happens.

Very little is written or talked about sibling relationships. Feelings about siblings are ultimately interpreted as feelings about parents. This is true in as much as parents are entirely responsible for creating our siblings and siblings (including the lack of them) affect our relationships with our parents hugely. But there's almost an assumption that sibling relationships have no developmental identity or therapeutic significance in their own right. I suspect that so many young people apply to be student counsellors (and they do) because on one level they want to repair something about their own sibling experience, either by doing what they didn't do at the time (being kind to younger siblings) or by offering others what they themselves didn't get at the time (being looked after by older siblings). Equally, younger students attach themselves to the student counsellors to get something they've not had or not had enough of in their own families.

Most of us begin with decidedly mixed feelings about any siblings we do have. We love them as the extensions of our parents and hate them as the people who get between us and our parents. Younger siblings are punishments as well as presents:

> I like the magic number 3
> the way it used to be,
> when 1 was Mum
> and 2 was Dad
> and 3 was only me. (J. Patrick Lewis 1992)

Managing such ambivalent feelings is difficult. Ambivalence is contradictory, after all. It doesn't make sense. Therefore it's easier for a young person to conclude that hating a sibling *so much* must invalidate any tender feelings she or he also has towards that sibling and mean that the hater is simply being a bad sister or brother. In counselling, young people are often able to explore feelings of hatred and anger towards a family member only once their feelings of love and concern for that person have first been acknowledged with the counsellor as equally real. Otherwise, they feel too guilty. Then the idea that it's normal to have mixed feelings about the very people we care most about comes as an enormous relief.

Relationships between student counsellors and younger students allow everyone to have another go, to express affectionate feelings towards someone a bit younger or someone a bit older. Winnicott (1965) writes about the baby's eventual feelings of guilt towards its mother on account of its own clawing neediness and about the baby's consequent need to make reparation. This making reparation manifests itself as 'concern', he says. The experience of guilt becomes the capacity for concern: we wouldn't feel guilty if we didn't care. So caring for her other children is one way of making it up to mother.

But it isn't easy. I think older students make amends for guilty family feelings by becoming student counsellors, thereby expressing the genuine concern they struggle to express in their own families. Otherwise, the nearest a sibling comes to a reparative relationship *within* the family might be with a pet, a substitute sibling to be cared for or confided in. Baby-sitting or looking after other people's animals might also be oblique ways of doing the same thing. Schools undoubtedly become mother-figures, ignoring or valuing their children's attempts to be 'good', so it's very important for the school to notice and publicly applaud its student counsellors' work. If, as Winnicott writes, 'there is no reliable mother-figure to receive the reparation-gesture, the guilt becomes intolerable, and concern cannot be felt' (p.82).

Writing years before Winnicott, Freud (1900) refers rather mysteriously to 'altruistic impulses and morality' awakening in children but also goes on to say that 'If this morality fails to develop, we like to talk of "degeneracy", though what in fact faces us is an inhibition in development' (p.350). Clearly the opportunity to develop exists at school for those relatively few people chosen to be student counsellors, but what of the hundreds of other young people never given such an opportunity? Are they simply left with stultifying, unproductive guilt? However much we talk about citizenship and social responsibility, schools don't find many ways for young people to take responsibility for others and yet for young people this may be a developmental *necessity*. How many teenagers have babies because they want to put right something they feel badly about in their lives? How many school leavers say they want to 'work with children'? I think there's a danger that young people are plunged into parenthood without first having had the *interme-diate* experience of looking after someone successfully while still not being ultimately responsible.

Because of this need to put things right, young people often idealise 'children', and there's potential for student counsellors and younger students to idealise one another. So the student counsellors are trained to think carefully about how they share their own experiences with younger students. While well-meaning stories about personal faults and failures ('Yes, that happened to me too!') can usefully demystify the student counsellors, some younger students need to believe in the ideal ('This person *really* understands and *really* cares about me') for a bit longer while their own hurts are being repaired as a result of *feeling* understood and cared for. But because this potential for idealisation exists, it's always important, as in any therapeutic relationship, for the student counsellors to end these relationships properly, gently but firmly giving back any lingering idealisations:

> 'We'll always be friends, won't we?'

> 'Well, we'll remember each other but we won't be meeting any more.'

When, the following year, a new team of student counsellors emerges, ready to do business, those younger students who got most out of the previous team appear not to notice at all. They never re-attach. They've moved on, having got what they needed.

I think a sibling's development might be described in three stages: as learning to acquire, maintain and share status. Like all stages of development these don't always follow a neat pro-gression and some young people get badly stuck. But secondary schools might broadly describe their new Year 7 students as struggling for the first year or so to acquire status, as working to maintain it thereafter, and in the later years of school as learning to share status with others, no longer in mortal dread of losing it.

The student counsellors represent this latter stage and, importantly, are able to model this sharing of status lower down the school, being seen to respect younger students as equally valuable human beings, remembering and calling them by their names, asking them about themselves, telling the younger students some things about themselves. The student counsellors make time for people. They're interested. Unlike older siblings, they don't envy younger students their lives. Rather, they see what a tough time many are having and respond accordingly. Precisely because they're *not* in real sibling relationships, ensnared by feelings of rivalry, they can offer a compassion which is more straightforward and gives younger students the support they're needing.

There are, after all, crucial things we learn from siblings which *can't* necessarily be learnt from parents. This includes how to play, how to express and resolve conflict, how to understand sexuality, how to manage privacy, how to measure personal achievement, how to cope with transitions and, perhaps most importantly, how to have a best friend. Usually these things are left to chance and young people muddle through. But some young people get stuck and this is where the student counsellors are on hand to help.

One of the things they do is to take turns to staff a room every lunchtime where younger students can come and talk in private about friends and enemies, families and other relationships. Lots of younger students use this facility. So it was interesting when a group of girls in Year 7 told their form tutor that they wanted to set up a classroom where they would be every lunchtime for people to come and talk with them about being bullied or being a bully. The model they were copying seemed obvious. What happened was that we assigned two student counsellors to them as 'consultants', so that the girls could feel their enthusiasm being affirmed while talking through the exact practicalities of what they were proposing.

Inevitably, family relationships from the past are revived in all groups. Other people remind us of our parents, brothers, sisters, and we sometimes respond to them accordingly. The leader of the group is set up to be the parent-figure, with group members idealising or loathing the leader in much the same way as siblings might respond to their parents.

This process happens in meetings, teams, classrooms – indeed, at some level, in all relationships. But what's sometimes underestimated is how much of importance goes on between the so-called siblings themselves. Although the focus is inevitably on the parent-figure when group members are dissatisfied or feeling helpless, it's important to recognise that this conveniently avoids group members looking at their relationships with each other. In groups I run, whether they're in educational or other settings, much of the learning, much of what's 'therapeutic' about the groups, consists in members' experience of each other: feeling supported for the first time, not being laughed at, finding out that other people feel similarly, being able to challenge people without reprisal. All this can correct or amend what's gone on before in a person's life. Any group needs a leader/parent to look after it initially, to hold members/ siblings safe until they can do more for themselves, and this job is crucial. But equally crucial is what happens thereafter, when the siblings, with the parent's help, begin to encounter each other.

Usually at this stage the group members are anxious to get on, to be accepted and liked, to make new, productive relationships, unconsciously aware of all the things that have been unproductive in their actual sibling relationships and keen for a fresh start. The student counsellors also run formal groups for younger students, using carefully thought-out structures to facilitate openness and sharing. This is sometimes called 'peer education' yet, when it works, it never is strictly *peer* education but consists, rather, of older students and younger students. What makes the groups work (apart from a lot of training and planning) is that some age difference is involved. The leaders are older brother- or sister-figures, thereby stimulating and fulfilling everyone's need for a reparative sibling experience. I remember when I worked in the youth centre how *badly* thirteen- and fourteen-year-olds wanted to help run discos for eleven- and twelve-year-olds. The waiting list would be long, often with the names of people who got into lots of trouble at school. They'd keep checking to see where their name had got to on the list, urging me to make an exception by promoting their name. Then when their turn did come to help with the next disco they'd be excellent, hugely committed to helping the 'little kids' have a good time, whereas on committees designed to involve young people in the overall running of the youth centre for *everyone's* benefit ('peer' committees) they'd be much more hesitant.

All but one of the teams of student counsellors I've managed myself have got on well together, supporting each other and enjoying each other's company. I haven't sought to tease out rivalries lurking between team members. Rather, I've encouraged people to collaborate and enjoyed their surprise when, after years in school of always seeing one another in set ways, they've woken up to the skills and qualities they never knew their new colleagues possessed. Being part of the team is a new start, a new family for everyone.

The team which didn't get on was interesting. They, too, made a fresh start with their old preconceptions about each other pushed to one side. They, too, were enthusiastic. What gradually undermined that enthusiasm, though, and allowed old rivalries and resentments to resurface was that, for various reasons, they had no shared working experience. Other teams have had a slot in the week when they've all come together to run something, usually a lunchtime session for younger students in the nearby youth centre. This has always served to demystify team members to each other. Rather than *imagine* someone else is more popular or more successful than you are with younger students, everyone can see for themselves and this makes it much harder to sustain jealous fantasies. They can also see for themselves who gets on best with me, the parent-figure.

Because of the part that parent-figures have to play in this process, all the teams of student counsellors I've known have been most effective when their work has been most closely structured and managed by an *adult*, with at least fortnightly team meetings to organise work and monthly supervision to discuss in detail the younger students they've been listening to. In some cases a second adult can provide the supervision but, either way, the parent-figure is playing his or her appropriate role, not abdicating responsibility to eldest sibling-figures but remaining ultimately responsible. Then the eldest sibling, given an *explicit* role and title, doesn't have to feel embarrassed or guilty about taking responsibility for younger siblings and sometimes failing.

In the school where I worked as the counsellor I remember many students whose first important conversations had been with a student counsellor who then, knowing his or her own limits, had suggested they see me. But in schools where everything is left entirely to the student counsellors and the adults back off, the student counsellors end up feeling resentful of their role and guilty about things never going to plan. It's too much. It's unfair to be expected *to parent* rather than just *to sibling* (as it were) younger people. Equally, in schools where there is little shared vision in the staffroom, where the school can't decide whether to follow the voices of law and order (often men) or the voices of care and sympathy (often women), the student counsellors are again caught in the middle, expected to work miracles. Like the children of warring couples, they end up resenting their own existence.

Perhaps because women are traditionally associated with caring roles, fewer boys than girls apply to be student counsellors. Sayers (1998) argues that, to prove their masculinity, boys separate more quickly from their mothers but then find themselves in frightening isolation. They compensate for this awful feeling of isolation with *grandiosity* ('I'm bigger, better, braver than you'), but remain fearful that this carefully constructed new world will collapse completely. I think boys are therefore reluctant to apply to be student counsellors, to have the title, the training, the expectation, *for fear of being no good*, of being unable to live up to something. Perhaps fathers suffer from the same fear. If it seems much clearer how to 'be' a mother than a father, then it may seem clearer how to be sisterly rather than brotherly.

In any case, boys and girls express their concern and their friendliness differently. One team of student counsellors was telling me about how in school you know you've made friends with another girl when she says, 'D'you want to come to the toilet with me?' Then you know you're accepted. We laughed at the thought of boys coping with such an invitation.

But one group of boys I was working with got round to complaining about the girls in their form. 'Girls don't understand boys,' they said. I asked what exactly it was that girls didn't understand. They hesitated. 'Well,' said one boy, searching, 'football!' I nodded, as if I knew what he meant. The other boys knew what he meant. There seems to be something about the language of football which equates with the language of relationships, where 'not passing' means not sharing, 'goal hanging' means taking all the credit, 'being on the same side' means being friends, and 'not knowing whose side you're on' means being caught between loyalties. The metaphors are many. And they're *enacted* every lunchtime on school playing fields. This, perhaps, is what the girls didn't understand.

Luke was a male student counsellor who didn't seem much interested in the bits of theory I proffered at team meetings. While the female student counsellors were keen to speculate about what was going on emotionally with the younger students, Luke said little. Yet he was beloved of many younger students, not because he happened to be captain of the school rugby team but because he *played* with them, joining in their football and other playground games. He did play-fighting. He arm-wrestled. He had few conversations explicitly about 'feelings' but *did* things instead, and younger students, especially boys, knew he was just as concerned for them as were any of the female student counsellors.

If masculinity is an outdated concept and masculinit*ies* a more useful way of thinking, then Luke epitomised one kind of masculinity. Simon epitomised another with his Glastonbury T-shirt and friendship bracelets. Dale was different again, more formal, smiling nervously as he chatted to younger students in the dinner queue. Jovan was a dude, Mikey was shy, Alan liked organising things. Boys just express their concern in all sorts of different ways. I wonder whether girls apply so readily to be student counsellors because they're expected from an early age to be little mothers in their families and, finding themselves wholly unequipped for the role, *hate* their siblings for the sense of inadequacy they're stuck with. So they desperately seek opportunities outside the family to try again.

Among the student counsellors I've worked with in one school in the last six years, 27 have been the eldest child in their family, 8 the middle child and 18 the youngest. I don't think there's anything very surprising about this. It suggests that eldest children, feeling displaced in their parents' affections and with an increased sense of responsibility because of their position in the family possibly have most need to make up for hating their younger siblings. What's interesting, though, is that there have been no 'only' children. This may be a complete coincidence or it may be because only children have no need to make up for anything or, alternatively, lack the confidence to act as sibling-figures. I'm certainly aware of only children, when they're younger, making plenty of rewarding relationships with student counsellors.

I worry with my supervisor about the term 'student counsellor'. Counsellors are adults, trained over many years. They have their own professional organisation. 'Student counsellor' usually refers to an adult counsellor working in further or higher education. But like parents who don't let the children know what's happening, counsellors shouldn't hoard the skills and insights they have. Other people can contribute as well. What goes on in the relationships between these student counsellors and younger students includes much that is *mutually* therapeutic, that heals or modifies old experiences and moves people on. In schools that seems important.

CHAPTER 3

Chloe

Understanding and Helping with Squabbles

The eight student counsellors are bemused. What they *don't* tell me is that this isn't what they had in mind when they applied for the job in May. Nor is it what they expected after their training during June and July: bullying maybe, and family problems for sure, but not constant tales of corridor squabbling.

'When we're in the counselling room at lunchtimes and people come in, all they want to talk about is their friends and who they've fallen out with recently. Like the other day, two of them came in to talk about a girl in Year 8 called Chloe, who they'd had some sort of falling-out with. And then ten minutes later Chloe and another girl came in, wanting to talk about *them*!'

They tell me all this half-accusingly, unsure whether it's adequate material for our supervision session or whether they're somehow failing in not providing me with more exotic problems to discuss about the younger students they've been listening to.

'Lisa and Becky said Chloe had been talking about them behind their backs, saying they were boring. So they asked her and she said she hadn't been saying anything at all but they still think she has.'

'And Chloe?'

'Chloe says she does think they're a *bit* boring but that she didn't say anything to anyone. She says they're going round now ignoring her and Rachel.'

'What did you say?'

'Nothing really. We just listened. There didn't seem to be anything *to* say. You can't ask them how they're getting on at home when all they want to do is talk about each other!'

Eight compassionate, resourceful seventeen-year-old people have committed themselves to this on top of all their A-level work: to listening a lot, befriending sometimes lonely students, trying to understand and bear something of other people's pain. We begin to talk about Chloe and her friends and the meaning of their story, and at the same time I'm reminded of teachers, youth workers and others also complaining of the pettiness of younger students with their nagging, trivial stories. I'm reminded of regular complaints – *They're really young for their age! They'll just have to grow up! I simply haven't time for all their squabbling!* And I'm reminded of my own inclination to dismiss the small concerns of younger teenagers as unnecessary and somehow as less engaging than the concerns of older, more obviously distressed young people.

I'm not surprised Chloe and her friends take up so much of the student counsellors' time because what is happening with them is actually central to the task of growing up. The story they tell is all about attachment and separation, liking and disliking, trusting and no longer being able to trust. First they came together as a group but now they're split into pairs and will, no doubt, go on to make other attachments, groupings and sub-groupings, pairings and threesomes in the weeks and months to come. What they're doing now is *practising* a series of roles, exploring a series of dilemmas. They *need* to practise and sometimes they practise frantically, trying out as many roles as possible. Then sometimes they get stuck. How *do* you tell someone you find them boring? Or that you like them in some ways and find them boring in others? Or that your feeling about them has changed? What happens when the person you thought liked you seems now to like someone else? When you realise that your best friend wants to be close to other people as well? How can you tell if someone really does like you? Which bits do they like? Which bits of yourself should you hide?

When they get home from school, I imagine Chloe and her friends switching on the TV soaps to watch, exhausted, as slightly older people wrestle with the same dilemmas they themselves have just spent their day in school trying to resolve. They'll notice how other people manage similar roles, similar conflicts, and they'll return to school next day to continue their own practising.

This matters because for most young people it is, in my experience, a consuming activity, the significance of which is usually lost in the swirl of the school day with its formal distractions and adult priorities. Because it's all around us we don't see it: young people trying out different roles, liking some, choosing some, resenting and struggling with others. Overworked teachers concentrate on crises and have little time left for the insistent, low-key anxiety of so many students trying out so many roles: trying out life itself. In schools the whole group usually feels too large and too complex to attend to, so as professionals we concentrate on the individuals and get peeved when groups such as Chloe and her friends seem to spend so much time apparently just squabbling. But the problem is that some young people get badly stuck in one particular role and need help from a teacher, a counsellor or, in this case, from student counsellors to enable them to move on.

These eight student counsellors may sometimes get frustrated but they do remain open to ideas and don't want their own frustration to affect Chloe and her friends. So together we try to make some sense of the story.

I was once sitting in a boring meeting during a school lunchtime. Through a window I was able to watch a group of Year 8 boys I knew spend the whole lunchtime (the *whole* lunchtime) play-fighting. Their play revolved around Matt, who spent the entire time tripping, cuffing, chasing and punching them. He was clearly Boss and his role was to put down rebellions. Paul was just as big as Matt but seemed resigned to his role as Number Two, never challenging Matt outright, though Matt threatened him constantly as if to pre-empt any challenge Paul might one day dare to make. The other boys' roles were as Irritants, wearily challenging Matt but also challenging Paul who had to put down his share of rebellions in order to remain Number Two. Years later, as it happens, Matt took up serious bodybuilding and Paul got into cars in a big way.

The boys may never have resolved or moved on from this particular fix. Before lunch they may have been comparing the Hindu and Buddhist religions. After lunch they may have gone on to read some Shakespeare – I don't know. But for almost an hour they looked well and truly stuck. I imagine them perhaps having different roles at home. I imagine Matt helping with his disabled sister or Paul staying moodily in his room. I imagine each Irritant having a series of roles particular to himself and probably quite different from the one role he found himself playing that lunchtime. J.L. Moreno (1972), the proponent of group psychotherapy, argues that 'Roles do not emerge from the self, but the self may emerge from roles' – in other words, we're each of us individuals but each made up of many different roles. We each have a role repertoire and that repertoire needs to be as large and as developed as possible for us to live creatively and healthily. Pitzele (1991) goes on to describe the variety and interconnectedness of the many roles we're each capable of playing. 'In short,' he concludes, 'each of us may be thought of as a group' (p.16).

I do an exercise on counselling skills training courses, explaining this to students. They must each write down three roles they've liked playing in their lives and three other roles they've not liked playing. They must then *cast* each role with only the other members of the course to choose from. Who'll play your irresponsible self, your hard-working self, your competitive self, your loving self? I explain that the way we feel about other people in the group will relate to how we feel about those same roles we ourselves play and which we've just ascribed to them. For we *project* the many aspects of ourselves on to other members of whichever group we happen to be in. We do it all the time. We can't help it. We see ourselves reflected in the people around us and, in part, we react to these people as we react to the parts of ourselves they've come to represent.

For example, I remember the early rehearsals for a rock musical I worked on with young people. Garry was cast as 'Stevie', the physically disabled member of a circus community. Garry was embarrassed to improvise the role in front of his friends, so I asked him to watch first: everyone in the cast then improvised the role simultaneously. They were all 'Stevie' for five minutes and spoke about how it felt. After this Garry was able to take on the role and played it with great humanity. It seemed that he'd been confronted and got stuck with his own feelings of disability, the *part of himself* which knew perfectly well what it might be like to be Stevie but couldn't perform the role in public. By making the role itself public and discovering that everyone could 'play' it, that this role was shared by other people too, Garry was freed to explore it for himself and (in performance) on behalf of the audience.

Some young people, however, become unable to play certain roles. They get stuck, often fixed in the effort to contain feelings. I worked as a youth worker with Martin for several years, until he was sixteen. Most mornings I drove past him on his way to school. He was always late, always walking *so* slowly, dragging his legs along, seemingly oblivious to the reprimands awaiting him at school. He never said much and in staff meetings teachers would vent their frustration at his apathy, his lethargy, his apparent disdain. I think the truth was that all Martin's effort went into containing an anger which no one, including me, was ever allowed to know about. In containing it, he was stuck in this all-consuming role except once a week on a Wednesday evening when we used to play football at the youth centre. Here Martin came to life, making up in bloody-mindedness what he lacked in skill. People always wanted him in their team because he was such an aggressive defender. In school he played his 'I Don't Care' role to perfection, but on the football pitch he could play a different (though undoubtedly linked) role of 'No One Gets Past Me'.

Depression is sometimes described as a defence against overwhelming feelings. Martin certainly wasn't clinically depressed. But some school students *are* monotonic, monosyllabic, their faces blank or stricken with perpetual anxiety. Sometimes they're called 'vacant', 'boring' or 'isolated'. They sometimes become the objects of bullying behaviour. What they seem to have, in Moreno's terms, is a limited role repertoire. Like Martin, they've got stuck in one role in order to contain or defend against certain feelings, but they may also have been given that particular role by others.

In this way, so much of Chloe and her friends' squabbling will derive from learnt family roles, now being re-enacted in school. The roles we internalise in early life are usually our most enduring. Sometimes they stand us in excellent stead but sometimes they prove inadequate to deal with our adult tasks. A counsellor recently described a young parent to me as 'someone desperately trying to do it differently but who has nothing to do it differently with'. Chloe and her friends, as young teenagers, are almost repeating the cries of young children, beseeching parents to *choose! choose! choose!* between siblings. So much of our role-taking as children is in response to the inevitable parental dictum, the awful paradox of *I love you the same but different.* In struggling to come to terms with that, we develop some of our most enduring roles: Attention-seeker, Fighter, Nobody Loves Me, Mummy's Little Helper, Daddy's Boy ...

Family therapy often looks at these roles as systemic: members of the family play interdependent roles *on behalf of* the whole family. Someone will play the role of Baby, someone the Delinquent, someone the Slave, someone else the Organiser and so on. If one part of this system adjusts itself, shifts, all the other parts must then make a corresponding adjustment or change. All groups, including family groups, have tasks to do. That task may be official (organising a holiday) or unofficial (not upsetting Dad), but either way there are things to be done and in mature groups people will take on and change roles according to what needs doing. But in an immature group, roles are clearly allocated and persist. Individuals get stuck and the group gets stuck. When the task changes the group can't then adapt.

I think this is when squabbling happens among young people such as Chloe and her friends. The role of Best Friend may have been an appropriate and necessary role for someone to play in the first year of secondary school in order to deal with the task of surviving and acclimatising in a strange environment. But a year or two later, survival is no longer the issue. The task has changed to one of exploration and the person who played the role of Best Friend must take on additional roles, additional uses. Where power becomes part of that exploration, someone will take on the role of Boss, for example. Someone will be Number Two. Someone else will take on the role of Joker or Brainbox, Peacemaker or some other role. One member of the group will almost inevitably take on the role of Punchbag, either because it's a role he or she is already accustomed to playing at home or because the group forces that role on to the person. Most groups set someone up in that particular role and spend a great deal of time attacking it. They project all their most uncomfortable, untrusted, inadmissible parts on to the Punchbag.

Most of us have had, however briefly, an experience of the Punchbag role in our lives. Most of us have escaped it because we've had other roles in our repertoire to escape to. But some people and some groups get stuck and need outside intervention to unstick them.

This process isn't necessarily confined to young people. In staffrooms, for instance, the same familial roles can be enacted with the same stubborn determination as Martin (p.38) held on to his role. One teacher is the Dutiful Child: reliable, never questioning, always working hard. Another is the Rebel. Another is the Incompetent, always forgetting things; another the Baby in need of constant looking-after. Others play the Loner, the Social Organiser, the Sulky Teenager, the Flirt, the Delicate Flower, the Warrior and so on. The headteacher takes on and is readily given the role of Parent, playing it the way he or she has experienced parents and sometimes, like a parent, resenting the role altogether. Deputy heads might be Eldest Children. Hagelthorn (1990) writes, 'A role requires a counterpart. The role of "Romeo" requires the role of "Juliet", the role of "parent" requires the role of "child", the role of "victim" requires the role of "oppressor" and so on' (pp.7–8).

Some roles exist within us because of our individual histories: we've already learnt them well, hence our predisposition to take them on. But they also exist in terms of the whole group because we can only play them in relation to other people already playing other roles. If the role of Angry Young Man has already been bagged, then the newcomer with a personal predisposition to that role will find himself inevitably being allocated something a bit different by the unconscious mind of the staffroom.

Perhaps teachers get so frustrated with people like Martin because his stuckness reminds them of their own. How many teachers dream of having other jobs! Yet how many, on in-service training courses, want to pack up and leave as soon as the trainer mentions the dreaded word, *role-play*! New roles are exciting, for sure, but frightening. If in our families we're allotted firm, clear, enduring roles then perhaps we come to school to try out all the roles our families won't allow. Surprised parents will then reply to complaining or to admiring teachers, 'Well, she's not like that at home!'; and even between lessons students may change roles: diligent in Physics, disruptive in French. Moreno (1961) again:

Everybody is expected to live up to his official role in life; a teacher is to act as a teacher, a pupil as a pupil, and so forth. But the individual craves to embody far more roles than those he is allowed to act out in life ... Every individual is filled with different roles in which he wants to become active and that are present in him in different stages of development. *It is from the active pressure which these multiple individual units exert upon the manifest official role that a feeling of anxiety is often produced.* (my italics, p.63)

So the eight student counsellors might well be sitting with me, playing their *official* role as responsible, listening, patient student counsellors, but within that role other, unofficial roles may be bubbling: the role of Dissident ('I don't agree with you!'), the role of Flatterer ('You're so right!'), the role of Sceptic ('What's this got to do with Chloe and her friends?'). I sit wondering who'll dare to depart from his or her official role? The same anxiety is evinced by Chloe and her friends. Officially they're all playing the role of Friend but within that role other varieties are seeking expression: roles such as Best Friend, Second-best Friend, Martyr, Judas, Enemy and so on.

Chloe and her friends squabble, experiment with roles and test the ability of their friendship group to contain such experiments. But they remain afraid that these experiments will cause the eventual disintegration of the group and I think this fear looms large. In schools there are always examples of people who were best friends but who no longer speak: their friendship could no longer contain their differences.

I've used the following structure to help small groups of friends move on from such a stuckness before their friendship explodes. Each person must tell each other person two specific things they like or admire about that person followed by one thing they don't. The rules are strict: there must be two parts good to one part bad and the two good must come before the one bad. In this way people can get used to hearing criticism without feeling they're being written off altogether. They can only bear the criticism when it's prefaced by at least as much praise. Young people will otherwise often defend against a perceived attack by giving up altogether: 'Well if that's what you think then there's no point in us staying friends!' And they're outraged when other people (particularly adults) confuse *them* with *their behaviour*. We say things to them like 'You're a liar! You're a thief!' or 'You're a bully!' to which their unspoken retort always seems to be 'That may be true, but can't you see that I'm much *more* than that? That's *one* of the roles I play. But I'm also kind, I'm a good brother, a hard worker in the shop, a loyal Chelsea supporter! Why can't you also see *those* parts of me?'

It's frightening to let people see parts of ourselves we've hidden. As a drama teacher I found myself spending more and more time on warm-ups, developing trust and group cohesion, sometimes without ever getting beyond warm-ups at all because it seemed and still seems so important that, until the group is safe enough, it's simply unfair to ask people to try out unfamiliar roles. Young people are playing certain roles all the time anyway. What stops them trying out *different* roles and extending their repertoire is the fear of being criticised. To try out something new and then feel humiliated only makes us retreat and determine to stick to what we already know. Sometimes, despite everything, young people do try out new roles cautiously, quietly, only for some well-meaning adult to seize on this very first experiment and subject it to a barrage of praise: 'That was really good the way you didn't answer back today! Well done!' or 'I saw you talking to Josie yesterday. That must have been the first time in ages! Keep it up!' I think sometimes it's important *not* to notice as young people tentatively try out unfamiliar roles.

Chloe and her friends take their conflict to the student counsellors because they know something has to shift. The student counsellors must contain the conflict by listening, by not being prescriptive, by making the conflict permissible, safe, so that it can continue to be talked about until something eventually does shift. Emunah (1995) writes, 'Once the adolescent experiences relief and mastery through the process of expression and containment of emotion, he or she is psychically freed to begin to tackle one of the developmentally critical tasks of this life stage: experimentation with roles' (p.166).

Smaller children also experiment all the time, but at a safe distance. Long games evolve whereby Barbies, Sylvanians or Action Men enact human conflicts, many of which get resolved. Some conflicts don't resolve themselves so easily though and, where the safe projective level can't be sustained, are taken to real-life parent-figures: 'She won't let me share her house!' or 'He's not playing properly!' I think then it's less important to find the perfect solution, even if one existed, than simply to contain the conflict, to find perhaps an interim solution which makes it possible to go on with the game without the roles becoming entrenched or losing their playfulness. The same principle underlies play therapy with abused children: using projective distance to make sense of things, to practise, to experiment.

Indeed it might be argued that all teenage relationships are merely the projections of the teenager. Joni Mitchell (1971) sings ruefully, 'I love you when I forget about me.' Rock bands have always served to hang our adolescent projections on: we love the Mad One, the Little One, the Hunky One, the Shy One; we hate the Tall One, the Weird One, the Boring One, the Mouthy One. The Spice Girls served wonderfully: each with her own distinct role in the group, inviting a million projections and a million ways for teenage girls to talk obliquely about aspects of themselves, roles they approve of and roles they mistrust. Bannister (1995) describes this shift: 'Projective play occurs when the child begins to discover the external world and to project feelings and stories onto toys and other objects. Role play develops as the child begins to make relationships and to use dramatic action to relate her inner world to the environment' (p.43). So with the Spice Girls: 'Mel B's good because she says what she thinks! Emma's okay but I don't like her pig-tails and I really hate Geri. She's a slag!'

Discos give young people a chance to practise roles which are scary because they're even closer to grown-up, sexual reality: amorous roles, marital roles, monogamous roles, unfaithful roles. Young people sometimes spend hours in their bedrooms preparing, just in order to be ready to practise. When they arrive at the disco they immediately check out their existing friends, making sure everyone's there who should be and comparing notes. This done, they begin to explore, dancing a bit in between dashing round a lot. 'Will you ask her out for me?' becomes a safe way of practising a role without going the whole way. As the evening progresses people experiment more daringly. Two people will be snogging, gawped at by others. Finally the slow dances will discover various couples in the half-light, hands placed respectfully but at the same time daringly on each other's buttocks.

This is important stuff. Discos endure because the need to practise these roles endures. A good disco gives young people an experience of coming together en masse that is fun and safe, without anyone wrecking things. But good discos, like good therapeutic groups, only happen when there are clear, understood rules with 'parent-figures' supervising and, where necessary, taking absolute responsibility for enforcing the rules.

Outside the disco, at the bottom of the road, among a group of older young people, there are no parent-figures and panic has set in. Adulthood is round the corner and the role-playing is manic. Someone's being sick into a bush. Dave and Natalie are in the middle of a two-minute kiss. Gaz is calling Jono a wanker and is about to hit him because of what Jono's supposed to have said about Alison and her sister. Dean turns the car radio up while Sophie and Emma sit in his back seat, smoking a spliff. Ginny stands nearby, fed up, waiting for her lift, wondering if she could be pregnant. She curses as the police car looms into view.

Now one of the student counsellors abandons her Deferential role and bursts into the role of Demagogue: 'I don't see how any of this is going to help us the next time we see Chloe and her friends! I mean, what are we supposed to *do*, apart from listen to their squabbling?'

Again I make my point about containment, about making it safe enough for Chloe and her friends to keep working on the problem themselves.

'Yeah, but what if they can't work it out for themselves?'

We talk about problem pages, how avidly they're read by teenagers and how useful they are in working with groups. The student counsellors could invent realistic problems and give them to Chloe and her friends to think about. The problems could be written down or described verbally but mustn't be *explicitly* about Chloe and her friends. As long as they're about Jasmin or Jo, Julie or Janice, the girls will engage. Problem pages are like toys in that we can play with them as if they were about ourselves but with ourselves kept at a safe, projective distance. Groups can themselves make up real problems and give them to other groups to advise on. In this way conflicts can be looked at from the outside and can be looked at differently because we step out of our stuck role as – in the case of Chloe and the others – Friend and take on a new role of Enlightened Observer.

The student counsellors are restless. This is all very well but how *do* you help someone develop a wider role repertoire?

In the groups I run for young people we sometimes do an exercise early on whereby each member of the group takes a turn in the spotlight. The person in the spotlight says and does nothing. Every other member of the group has to say aloud one thing he or she imagines to be true about the person in the spotlight *but doesn't already know for a fact*. When everyone has said something, then the person in the spotlight has a chance to respond, saying as much or as little of the 'truth' as he or she chooses. 'You're right about me not liking this school when I started. I hated it. But it's not right that I don't get on with my brother. We don't speak a lot but we do get on.' The group's assumptions are clarified in this way and individuals begin to be freed from predetermined roles in the group because they're able to bring in new parts of themselves and other roles they play outside the group. But the person in the spotlight reserves the right not to say very much at all, and this is important because one of my aims for the group is to help its members respect and understand each other's defences, not destroy them. It might be important to accept shyness, for example, as a learnt way of dealing with frightening situations. When the shy person feels safe enough, he or she may begin to experiment with other roles, other responses to life.

Another favourite exercise is this guessing game. One person sits with his or her back to the others. Secretly, the others decide which member of the group they're going to describe and the person with his or her back to the group must guess who it is. The group members then call out things about the person they're describing but must only call out positive things about that person. What appears to be a simple guessing game is actually a way of helping people say the positive things about one another they would otherwise never get round to saying. Again, we're freed from stuck roles, from our limited repertoire of responses, when we feel valued and therefore safer.

When the group is ready and can cope, another guessing game involves role reversal. 'Be someone else in the group. Don't tell us who you've chosen to be. Answer our questions as if you were that person and we'll eventually try and guess who you are.' Once the group has guessed correctly, the person portrayed can correct any misrepresentations. The aim is for each person to have a go at *playing someone else* while everybody else is wondering, Could that be me? The game just loosens the fixed roles a little.

I also use an exercise where, with the group sitting in a circle, two chairs are placed one behind the other. Someone sits in the front chair and speaks about him or herself as they think others see them. 'People see me as confident, good at school work, able to get on well with people, got lots of friends.' The same person then moves to sit in the chair behind and speaks about him or herself *as they really are.* 'Actually I get really nervous. I always think people don't like me and I find a lot of my school work really hard, which is why I don't always come out in the evenings because it takes me so long to do it.' I tell the rest of the group who are sitting in the circle to stay where they are if they themselves can relate to some part of what the person's just said and, if not, to get up and stand behind their chairs. The person who's been speaking can then choose one member of the group still sitting to explain what it is he or she relates to and why.

In this way the onus is on group members to share experiences simply because it requires more effort not to. Apart from using this methodical structure to help people share, my idea is that when we're stuck in a role we often feel isolated. Finding out that other people do share our feelings potentially frees us to move on because we're no longer so alone.

In a group that's been running for a while and has become safe enough, young people will look directly at the very situations they know they get stuck with. I offer this as an opportunity to *practise* for real life, setting up these situations in order to try things out, and using other members of the group to play roles for us. What we often do first, though, is to take a series of prescribed situations (as with problem pages) and, working in pairs, show the rest of the group first the 'wrong' way of handling a given situation and then what the pair considers to be the 'right' way of handling it. We discuss this. But what's important is being allowed to do it the 'wrong' way first, partly because it's fun but also because it gives permission for the two people to take on radically different roles. They can be Insensitive, Bloody-minded, Pathetic, Thoughtless, Weedy, Loud,

Indecisive, Cruel ... all those parts of themselves, those roles they've always wanted, but never had the chance, to try out. And in my experience, having this opportunity to try out, say, a Cruel role in the safety of the group makes it *less* likely that a person will need to take on that role in real life at other people's expense.

The student counsellors have had enough. They look as if they're thinking about all the roles they never get to play. Being supportive and responsible for other people is fine for six and a half hours a day but it's tiring, and now it's Friday and everyone else has already left school. They say goodbye and leave to go home and eat, to play tennis, to go to the doctor's, to go to work at the pub, to get ready for going out, to do more coursework, to go to a band rehearsal, to visit a friend in London...

CHAPTER 4

Are We Like You?

Strangers and Strangeness

There's an old story about a son growing up in a poor country who reluctantly says goodbye to his parents and sets sail to seek his fortune. Many years go by. Eventually the son, by now a rich man, decides to return to his homeland but his ship is wrecked at night in a storm.

His parents are by now very old and poor and despairing of ever seeing their son again. Having heard a storm in the night, they go out as soon as it's daylight to see if anything valuable has been washed ashore. They find all sorts of things from a wrecked ship but it's the law in their country that people can only keep what they find from wrecks if there are no survivors. So when they come upon the body of a man, barely alive, lying face down in the sand, they take a huge rock and kill him. Searching for his purse, they turn the body over and see the face of their long-lost son.

The story remains powerful because it's about our need to leave home and our powerful fear of then returning home *and not being recognised*, of becoming a stranger. Young people know this fear and it disturbs them. Now that I'm older, now that I have my own interests, will Mum and Dad lose interest in me? If I'm not at home so much, am I deserting them? Will they therefore desert me? Or will I still have a place in their hearts? Jacey says that when she got home from a fortnight at her Dad's, her Mum called her a stranger. These things matter. It's difficult, for example, when an older sibling's bedroom is given over to a younger:

'It's my bedroom!'

'But you're not here any more!'

'So? It's still mine!'

In order to move on, young people need to know that their original place is secure and will remain so, that they can go back home when they need to, that they can curl up small and know someone will be there for them. Being sure of this means they don't then have to return constantly to check.

Some young people are safe in the knowledge that this is so and that they're free to go off and explore. But for others, home is by no means so safe and the strangeness of the world is therefore much more frightening.

'I feel like a stranger in my family,' says Linton. He leans forward, gazing at the floor. He's never met his Dad. His Mum drinks bleach sometimes and has to be accompanied by Linton to hospital in the ambulance whilst being sick. To the outside world, Linton appears to be taking all this in his stride, but inside he despairs. This is happening too soon. He's not ready: 'I feel like a stranger in my family.' My guess is that he's had to become *like a stranger* in order to cope, separating his own fear and anger from the situation, keeping it locked away. The fact that he's fifteen, wondering what will become of himself while struggling with coursework and friends, isn't recognised by his Mum and certainly not by his Dad. So in counselling we spend time recognising what it's like to be fifteen. Each week when he comes for his session Linton returns from the world of strangers to a room that's the same as he left it, where he can retreat, curl up and talk for a while before it's time to venture out again. He knows he shares the counselling room with others but that doesn't seem to matter as long as his own place in it is guaranteed, once a week. Here he's recognised. He's no longer a stranger.

Yet the story of the stranger on the seashore is also about our fear of not recognising or, more particularly, not understanding other people. Enigmatic, unnerving strangers abound in fairy-tales and legends and in modern stories such as Clint Eastwood's spaghetti Westerns. It's unclear whether they come to harm or to help. Linton himself struggles to recognise the strangers who are his parents. He knows he's connected to them but they don't make sense. Talking about the confusion he feels, however, means that he doesn't necessarily have to *enact* those feelings at his own or anyone else's expense. He doesn't have to kill anyone.

At times young people feel themselves to be strangers in the world and at other times they see strangers and strangeness all around. 'Strange' is the word they use to hint at a whole area of experience and wonder. Strange is familiar yet somehow different. Strange is feeling alone even though there are other people around. Strange is the way things don't make sense like they used to. Strange is how it feels to be emerging into independent adult life while still having dependent, childlike needs. Strange is what it was like, Kerry tells me, 'when we knew Dad had left home but for a whole week no one told us'. Some young people use the word a lot, while for others it translates as 'weird'. 'Weird' and 'strange' are interchangeable and are key words in the vocabulary of most young people. Sometimes they're used as insults, aimed at those who stand accused of being different, and sometimes they take the place of 'numb', meaning 'I don't know what I feel ... I don't know why I feel like this.' But 'strange' and 'weird' always allude to some kind of hiatus, some experience which doesn't make sense. 'New Year was weird,' says Hannah, on a cold January morning. 'It's like looking back at all the things that have happened and looking forward to the future and having really positive thoughts but not knowing what will happen. That's weird!'

I think that whenever young people describe the strangeness of the world they're currently experiencing they allude, in part, to some original attachment from which they're in the process of separating. 'I don't feel *at home* at home,' complains Mary. They're describing the feeling of *estrangement* from a child's world and from an original secure relationship. 'Strange' is how the world looks when we peep out from behind Mum. The big world says 'Boo!' – which is really scary but always exciting. So we peep out again.

This new world is fascinating, which is why we'll eventually give ourselves over to it, but it's also frightening, which is why we'll continue to mourn the loss of that original relationship. Hamed, for example, keeps walking out of school but he always comes back and, despite getting into lots of trouble at school, never does quite enough to get himself permanently excluded. He seems to depend on school as much as he tries to escape it: walking out and walking back express that. I ask about his family at home. 'They're weird!' he remarks, crossly. I think it's his best way of describing what the conflict feels like as he struggles between an attachment to his family and the free choice he's begun to exercise. Like any young person, he wants it both ways.

Free choice is what most young people have been campaigning for all their lives. Suddenly exercising that choice in education, in a first job or at university isn't so simple. It's nerve-racking. And the idea of a relationship, which at home might have consisted of straightforward, hedonistic demands satisfied or not satisfied, becomes, when it's a matter of choice and negotiation between peers, a much more complex, strange thing. 'I think "friends" is an overused word,' muses Kayleigh. 'I mean, you never know who's going to be a real friend.'

When young people leave home they usually take with them carefully chosen objects to ease the transition: teddy bears, CDs, photos. When Adam left for university he took nothing. 'It's a fresh start,' he said. Knowing how deeply he'd always been involved in school and in his large community of friends, I was surprised. I wondered whether taking important reminders with him felt confusing, so it was safer simply to take nothing. I met him again at the end of his first term. He'd been back once after a month, he said, to collect some CDs and clothes from home. I asked how the first term had been. He paused. 'Different!'

'Strange' or 'weird' or 'different' is young people's awareness of things out there, separate from themselves:

> Are we like you?
> I can't be sure.
> As the sea as it turns,
> We are strange in our world. (Supergrass 1995)

For a baby unable to speak, strange is no longer being a physical extension of mother but being separate. When it's time to separate further, I think adolescents re-experience this feeling of estrangement and adults, too, especially at times of loss, experience it at intervals in their lives. It can be very frightening. In Camus's famous novel *L'Étranger* (1942) the narrator describes a mechanistic world, full of colour and people, but a world from which he seems detached, his feelings and intentions unclear. Significantly, the novel begins with the simple, short sentence, 'Mother died today.' We never find out whether this is the point, whether the narrator is like this because, separated from mother, the world has become altogether different. Now he speaks of 'the benign indifference of the world'. Now life is dictated by chance and choice.

Young people worry about chance and choice. They're intrigued by ethical dilemmas and by things that are strange or weird in everything from Harry Potter to *The X-Files*. When Shakespeare's young people contemplate the strangeness of the world, they see differing things. Miranda excitedly celebrates a 'brave new world' full of wondrous people, presided over by a benevolent father, while Edmund scorns with atheistic zeal the 'excellent foppery of the world' where, as soon as anything goes wrong, people deny personal responsibility and start blaming the gods. Although the young people I know also fluctuate between idealism and cynicism, most are cautiously agnostic. They want to believe in a protecting parent-figure who takes ultimate responsibility and makes sense of everything, but they won't identify themselves with the hard and fast truths of organised religion.

Not knowing can be uncomfortable, however. So sometimes when young people call someone else 'strange' they're actually referring to a part of themselves they're not sure about or can't acknowledge: 'People are strange when you're a stranger' (The Doors 1967). Robin, for example, visited the youth centre sometimes and tried to join in whatever was happening. He was autistic. Sometimes he shouted at himself and sometimes he hit himself. But he was friendly and most young people accepted him although they thought he was 'strange'. For them, 'strange' seemed to describe something between the familiar and unfamiliar because in a sense they also hit and argued with themselves, but whereas they successfully internalised their fighting, Robin couldn't. He was different.

A few of them despised him, however. Kristeva (1991) argues that we become anxious about strangers because there exists an unconscious presence, a shadow within ourselves, that we see far more readily in other people. By recognising the stranger within ourselves, we no longer have to be scared by the strangeness of others. For this reason I think it's important to encourage young people to talk more about the strangers and strangeness they experience, to delve, to begin to articulate the conflicts they wrestle with. The alternative is for them to act strangely, behave like strangers and, most cruelly, to attack strangeness in other people.

I remember working with a group of boys who were involved in homophobic bullying. During our second session I asked each boy, when it was his turn, to pick a card from my pack, read out the statement on it and comment before letting other people have their say. The statements were deliberately provocative, covering a range of subjects. By chance Louie, who I knew was a chief instigator of the bullying, picked out the card I'd inserted about homosexuality. He read it out: 'Being gay is unnatural.'

I waited for Louie to tell us all why he thought this was undoubtedly true.

'There's nothing wrong with being gay! I completely disagree. It's people's own business. You can't say what's natural! Who's to say what's natural?'

And the others, of course, all agreed with him.

The mismatch between what the boys thought and how I knew they behaved was clear. I think their *feeling* was that being gay was different, therefore strange, therefore frightening. Their thinking, on the other hand, was quite different and the two weren't connected. The same mismatch is evident when young people insist, 'I'm not racist!', yet are quickly involved in racist behaviour. Calling someone 'strange' or 'weird' refers, I think, to feelings and thoughts not yet fitting together: childlike fear with adult-like understanding. But the most important way to help the child catch up with the adult is not to teach the young person to recite politically correct attitudes but to pay more attention to the childlike feelings hidden away nervously inside. Only when we feel safe ourselves can we tolerate uncertainty in others. Only when we feel good about ourselves do we begin to value others. Only when our own feelings of strangeness are accepted as perfectly ordinary can we accept the strangers all around us.

In the boys' fourth and final session I added an empty chair to the circle. Whoever had the chair on his right side could invite another member of the group to come and sit next to him, for a reason. Having heard the reason, the invited person could move if he thought it was good enough or stay put if not. Whenever someone moved, his old chair became vacant and another person had the chance to invite someone to sit next to him. Tentatively, the boys began to invite one another and began to move. 'I want you to come and sit here because you're a good laugh ... Come and sit next to me because you let me copy your homework ... because you're a mate ... because we both support Man U.' Several people invited Louie to sit by them for these reasons and Louie, in turn, invited his particular friends to sit by him. The group was relaxing, intrigued as to who would be invited next and who would next have the empty seat by him. I invited Louie to sit by me because, I said, although his teasing of others in the group had annoyed me at times, I liked him a lot as a person. Louie moved. Later he took his cue: 'Brian, I'd like you to sit by me because I know I get on at you sometimes but you're not a bad bloke really.' There was a moment's silence. Brian shifted awkwardly. 'Okay!' He walked across the circle and sat down next to his tormentor. The group breathed again.

CHAPTER 5

Accidents
What Happens in School When There Are No Answers

Elaine and Assia were running across the main road one night when a car hit and killed Elaine. Weeks later, a coroner concluded that Elaine's death had been an accident.

Now Assia sits opposite me in a counselling room. She's thirteen. It's almost a year since her friend was killed. She can't stop feeling guilty, she says. Last week she cut her wrist and had to go to hospital. If, as the coroner said, what happened wasn't the driver's fault and wasn't her fault and wasn't Elaine's fault, then whose fault was it?

In blaming herself, Assia actually makes a kind of sense of what happened. If she'd been looking out for Elaine they'd have seen the car coming and the accident wouldn't have happened. *Someone* must have been to blame – otherwise, it doesn't make sense; otherwise, it *was* an accident and that's actually the worst thought because that means anything could happen. Assia winces. 'That's pointless,' she says, and then, 'I definitely should have seen the car.'

To believe that accidents really do happen is extremely hard. It means all sorts of things. It means that certain things in our lives just *happen*; that, despite our best attempts, ultimately we can't control the world or the future. Perhaps hardest and most disturbingly of all, it means we can't control death, which in turn means wondering why we bother to do what we do whilst we're alive.

Assia tells me she doesn't talk much to her family nowadays because she doesn't want to burden them. They have their own troubles, she says. Eventually she wants to be a primary teacher; she's always loved little kids. I find myself wondering whether Assia is turning herself into the eternal protector now, to compensate for not protecting Elaine a year ago. If so, it'll be important to work with her on whether Elaine's death really was Assia's fault and she therefore has to make up for it, or whether what happened could have been a genuine, inexplicable, pointless accident: in short, whether accidents *are* possible. Otherwise, at some point in the future Assia will discover that she can't protect the whole world and will then feel quite worthless.

The future looms large for young people. It's unknown and frightening. Accidents could happen. So education offers young people instead the idea of a future that can be controlled, that can be safe and fulfilling thanks to hard work and obedience. But this other future exists which can never be controlled and which can never be known; a future where accidents happen and we all eventually die. What if young people come to school already well aware of this other future? How much disruptive behaviour in schools, then, actually expresses an internal panic, a beseeching question: *What will become of me?*

So much school time is devoted to certainties, to passing on all the things adults have learnt and can prove. We distract young people from thinking too much about the most important things: all the questions for which ready-made answers are hard to find. We want them to feel safe. We want to spare them the awfulness of not knowing. But it may be our own adult anxieties we're sparing, anxieties about *our* futures and our children's futures independent of us. As Phillips (1995) writes, 'we acknowledge that the future cannot be guaranteed; and then we set out to guarantee it' (p.52).

I'm not suggesting for one minute that schools should abandon the safety of structures and rules in the interests of philosophical enquiry. Some questions certainly do have answers, just as some school rules can never be negotiable. But other questions may not have such ready answers. They're the questions everyone has to negotiate in their own way and in our interactions with young people we need to provide opportunities for this process to happen. I sometimes wonder how much a good school might actually be judged by the popularity of its RE department. To what extent can and do young people get to ask big questions? And how acceptable is this in the culture of the school? Because if adults sometimes lament the fact of children knowing too much too soon, saying children have lost a sense of awe and mystery, then it must be because it's been coached out of them. If children begin with a sense of mystery about things like dying, they lose it all the more quickly if we brutalise it with Answers.

In GP surgeries there's an assumption that ailments have cures, which is why it's so maddening to be told you've got 'a virus' and nothing can be done. In schools too there's an assumption that questions have answers: that is, students have questions and teachers have answers. And as people walk into a counselling room, there's also an assumption that cures and answers are somewhere in the vicinity. In some ways counselling tends to deal with the past, with what's already happened, with what can be known. But for young people counselling must also account for a future that can never be known, because that may be where a much greater anxiety is focused. What if accidents do happen?

Jaz sits in my counselling room in school, distraught. His girlfriend has dumped him for someone else and Jaz's world has collapsed. For Jaz this is no exaggeration. He says he feels empty, invisible, useless, as if the best of him has been thrown scornfully away. Of course there's a background story and, as the weeks go by, we'll explore it: the uncertainty he's always felt, the reasons why he came to invest everything in Laura in the first place. But for now no words are comforting; nothing can make sense of or heal his wound. All I can do is accept his tears, his emptiness and, in the weeks to come, his anger.

At the end of our session Jaz gets up to go, disappointed that I can't get Laura back for him but at least knowing his despair is being taken seriously. He goes off to his next lesson, disillusioned, having lost faith in life's essential fairness. Writing about religious disillusionment, the theologian Don Cupitt (1984) says, 'the only way to a first-hand personal faith is always through what many people call "the loss of faith". You have to go through inner turmoil; you have to descend into primal chaos, into that nameless region in the depths of the human soul where all meanings are unmade and remade' (pp.16–17). Whilst I'm not suggesting that young people like Jaz be expected to spend nights naked on Dartmoor, baying at the moon, I do think it's important that young people be allowed at least to question things and to *not know,* without adults nervously force-feeding them answers. Not knowing is a perfectly healthy state of mind.

In a famous letter, the poet John Keats (1817) described 'Negative Capability, that is when a man is capable of being in uncertainties, Mysteries, doubts, without any irritable reaching after fact & reason'. Keats even described 'the intense pleasure of not knowing'. But however desirable, it's distressing nevertheless to watch young people like Jaz wrestle with this. It might be pleasurable for a poet but it's hard work for most young people and their carers. Parents know they can never protect their children from all eventualities, and that knowledge is horrific. Children are always finally alone as they take the next big step forward, as the door closes, as the bus moves off. And like parents, teachers also have to let go constantly, never really knowing what will become of each person they've cared about. When those people in later life don't appear to have made the best use of what they've learnt, teaching can seem like a very pointless activity.

Becker (1973) describes the sense in which counselling frees people to live more honestly, only for that honesty to uncover despair at the heart of our existence. 'When you get a person to emerge into life, away from his dependencies, his automatic safety in the cloak of someone else's power, what joy can you promise him with his burden of aloneness?' (p.59). The honest answer to the question, of course, is 'None.' But young people *know* that. It doesn't surprise them. They may not like it but they know it to be true. Even Snakes and Ladders teaches that we're never safe: accidents can and do happen all the time. 'Only megalomaniacs make promises,' jokes Phillips (1995, p.53). Certainly a parent saying, 'I promise I'll always be there for you,' must worry the child who, because she or he knows about death, knows such a promise can't be kept. Children *want* promises because, like adults, they want to feel safe. Teenagers frantically promise each other love and friendship 4 ever but inside they're panicking.

Becker argues that we're born, like animals, with an innate knowledge and fear of death which haunts and torments us. Whether this is so or whether we acquire such a fear through early experiences of separation doesn't really matter. 'Death' might mean a variety of frightening things. But clearly the infant with its perpetually out-of-control body knows something about the physical self which the trained child chooses to forget, and that may be something about abandonment, aloneness, *accidents*. With our encouragement the child learns to avoid accidents. No sensible person would want to be reminded of those awful, out-of-control feelings. The belief systems, the material distractions we create to avoid such feelings are endless and they do a good job: they take our minds off the things we dread most until one day the illusion is shattered.

In the school where I worked as the counsellor, two students died one year. Working with some of their friends, it was important to help them voice lots of questions and *not* to have the answers. 'Why do people die? Why do they sometimes die young? What was the point of knowing them? Is death the end? What will become of us? What should we do now?'

The friends look at me, expecting answers. I say I don't know. They look puzzled, then sigh, almost with relief. At last! It seems that not knowing doesn't matter as long as *together* we don't know, because there are hundreds of other questions as well ... 'Why did Mum and Dad have me? Why did they split up so soon after I was born? Why did I get bullied? Why doesn't anyone want to go out with me?' We can and we do think about possible answers but there comes a point when we end up not knowing. Sometimes, I tentatively suggest, people *don't* know why they do things. Sometimes things happen by accident. The world may not be as organised as we imagine and therefore what happens may not be as personal or as persecutory as it sometimes feels.

The student counsellors in Year 13 whom I supervise often return from conversations with younger students confessing, 'I didn't know what to say! I felt completely stuck!' They blame themselves for not having a nicely turned homily for every occasion. I tell them that, on the contrary, they may be successful *because* they don't know what to say. It means they don't lie. It means younger students can know their concerns really *are* problematic, really *are* as dumbfounding as they feel. That much may be reassuring.

I'm not advocating that schools become places of relentless ignorance or that people should hold back when they have something useful to offer one another. The adult who deliberately says nothing may well just be a reminder of the inaccessible parent who never would engage with our distress in the first place. But the object of counselling isn't merely insight. Understanding how and why things happened is always useful but that, in a way, is the easy bit. It doesn't necessarily change the way we feel about ourselves or others and it doesn't necessarily take away the pain of the past or the dread of the future. Rather, we start to feel differently about things as new and different relationships (including the relationship with a counsellor) emerge in our lives, amending our past experience. We learn to manage old feelings, including feelings about the future.

This requires patience on the part of the counsellor. On counselling skills courses I run most people enjoy the getting-to-know-you exercises. They listen attentively and nod when I describe various listening strategies, but when we get to the role-play suddenly an anxiety sets in about not having answers. When, at the end of his story, an imaginary client inevitably concludes, 'I don't know what to do!', the practising counsellor turns away, panicking, 'I don't know what to say! I'm not supposed to give advice, am I? Oh God, I'm not doing this very well!' Almost always we ask the imaginary client for feedback about what the counsellor has done well so far. The client says, 'She's listening to me. She's not judging me. She seems interested.' I ask the client whether it matters that the counsellor hasn't come up with a solution. Usually the answer is an emphatic 'No: what's important is that she's there for me, she's listening.' *Occasionally* the answer is 'Yes, I do need some practical suggestions', and therein lies the skill of the counsellor in knowing when and how to offer those suggestions. But more often our skill lies in recognising and resisting our own anxiety, in believing that listening and accepting are often the best we can offer. In other words, it's not what you say ...

Nor is it what advice you give. Most of us are only too happy to be told what to do. The problem comes when the advice backfires, either because it never fitted our particular situation in the first place or more probably because we come to resent the fact that we've put ourselves in a dependent position, asking for advice. We knew what to do all along. We just needed someone else to know how frightening the responsibility felt.

Taking responsibility for the future (the thing we tell children they must do) is terrifying once we admit that the future really is uncertain. In a sense we're trying to control something that never will be controlled. We can *pretend* that the future's within our control, that exam qualifications will see us through, or money, God or a thousand insurance policies. But beneath the façade we know differently. For some young people gambling, drinking or risky drug-taking might be ways of dealing with this existential dilemma: surrendering to fate, refusing absolutely to take personal responsibility when faced with an underlying sense of life's futility. 'What difference does it make?' young people are fond of saying. The extent to which they blame adults and the world for everything is also the extent to which the arbitrariness of life terrifies them:

> I, a stranger and afraid
> In a world I never made. (A.E. Housman 1956)

It's as if adults should be making everything all right. Adults should be making life less hard, the future less frightening. When we have a near-accident we say, wistfully, 'Somebody must be looking after me!' The more young people waste time, the more rude and self-destructive they become, the more their anger seems to glare at us. But what they often keep hidden inside is guilt. I think young people know adults can only do so much and that in the end they have to take responsibility themselves. They're secretly sorry for behaving so badly, but personal responsibility can feel very frightening and very lonely.

Clinically, I've always struggled with when and how to 'allow' the suicidal thought. Young people mention suicide either angrily, sometimes to shock me, or embarrassedly, often after an overdose when they've recovered and been made to feel guilty. I wonder, will talking with a young person about his or her imagined suicide, imagined funeral, imagined funeral speeches and so on *confirm* that person's intention, making suicidal action more possible, or will it make the hitherto unacceptable, unspoken thought more bearable for being expressed and therefore *less* likely to be enacted? I tend towards the latter assumption, believing that we all share a suicidal *curiosity* which is really a curiosity about death, about our own worth and the meaning of our brief lives.

My dilemma about this is really the same dilemma about how and when to address a young person's sense of meaninglessness. Being *told* that life is meaningless, as a cult leader might finally tell his obedient disciples, is quite different from being given permission by a counsellor to wonder and keep wondering about such things, learning in the process to manage a really deep anxiety while continuing to enjoy all the distractions life offers. The anxiety is always there. The counsellor's dilemma is in judging when a young person can cope with overtly acknowledging it, because now may be too soon. One young person I worked with, Simon, whose father had died two years earlier, explained his father's death as *It was meant to be.* That seemed an understandable compromise between the idea of a benevolent, organising spirit who supplies meaning to events and the idea of a fatalistic, mechanistic world spinning out of our control. For the time being, this was Simon's understanding, his best way of coping.

As we grow older we accrue more and better defences. Like Simon's defence, these are precious. Sometimes people think of defences as a problem; that the defended person is cussed and narrow and that the aim of a counsellor is to break down defences. This isn't so. Defence mechanisms are hard-won. They usually exist in direct proportion to the degree of hurt they protect. We need them because when they fail we become frightened and chaotic again. Sometimes with young people it's necessary to identify, reinforce and even *celebrate* defences, seeing them as friends rather than foes. The problem with defences comes when they take on a life of their own and we find ourselves no longer using them just for protection. The task of the counsellor is then to notice the habitual defence and wonder with the client about the job the defence is doing. What occasioned that defence in the first place? Why has it developed so powerfully? Is it still doing the job it was originally created to do or have things moved on and is its usefulness therefore passing?

That time may have come when a person no longer feels satisfied with certain of his or her everyday behaviours. Charlotte is an A-level student of whom much is expected, not least by herself. She works almost every minute of the day but still it never feels enough. She sets herself extra work but that never gets finished. She says she doesn't think about the future or what it will be like if she gets the A-level grades she needs, and her achievements in the past give her no comfort either.

We talk. There are important family voices in her head, urging her on, but it seems that the huge wall of work she's erected for herself defends her especially against the unknown: as if by doing all this work she *will* be getting her A-level grades. This way, nothing can go wrong. Sitting the actual, unknown exams becomes irrelevant. Charlotte's unconscious belief is that by perpetual working she can guard against all uncertainty. *She can control her own destiny.* Yet this powerful belief is set against an insidious, insistent, conscious knowledge that she *can't* control her destiny and this is where Charlotte's distress seems lodged. She's terrified of what she knows she can never control. Spontaneously she refers to 'the pit', meaning the despair she feels when the defence isn't working, as it never entirely is. She says she doesn't need advice from people but rather someone to get into the pit with her, to stay and not leave her on her own. Her pit does seem terrifying yet the more we talk about it, exploring its recesses, its nooks and crannies, the more bearable it seems to become and, as the weeks go by, her need to defend against it with overworking diminishes. She can rest a bit.

Charlotte controls her fear with obsessive academic work in the same way as someone else might use food obsessively to create the same illusion of control, to manage the same terror. I suspect that big crowds cheer on their favourite teams so passionately because at some level they believe their support can affect the result, rather like encouraging a sick person – 'Come on! You can do it!' When the team loses, the crowd's disbelief is enormous, almost as if someone has died. Each defeat is a reminder that we can't control the destiny of other people and yet we return to the same stadium each week, refusing to believe this and, when the team does win, our belief in our omnipotence is restored.

Young people return from weeks camping in Welsh wildernesses tired and hungry but almost invariably having had a great time. I think this is partly because on mountain-tops people *share* an unspoken sense of individual and communal uselessness in the face of wind, rain, snow, danger. The fact that the experience is shared is what makes it thrilling and different. Rather than secretly, silently feeling powerless to deal with our own lives, we have it actually confirmed on a mountain-top. We *are* powerless! All of us! And that, of course, is thoroughly invigorating.

It's when we're on our own that any sense of futility is most appalling. When teachers begin to question who they are and what they're doing, sometimes towards the end of a career, they often lose confidence in teaching altogether and want to do something else. 'Knowing who you are means telling people what to do,' suggests Phillips (1995, p.6). I was part of a support group for teachers which ran for four years. During that time about 24 teachers used the group and over half of them either left the school or left teaching during or soon after their time in the group. It seemed that, through the group, they discovered to their amazement other people also questioning things. The group validated this questioning and, in so doing, gave people confidence to make changes, no longer believing themselves to be failures or peculiar.

Shakespeare's Hamlet also faces a whole series of questions and uncertainties. But again, when he despairs no one will share his despair. Other people stick to the particular modus vivendi they've settled for and no one will get into the despairing pit with Hamlet, not even his best friend. What's sometimes forgotten about Yorick's skull is that Yorick wasn't just anybody but someone who'd been an important father-figure when Hamlet was growing up. So holding the *skull* of a person who mattered that much and who cared about him brings Hamlet right up against a reality we shy away from nowadays, with our sanitised cremations, our euphemisms and determined distancing of death. In previous centuries it wasn't possible to avoid the physicality of death in ways we do now, nor is it possible in many poorer countries. Depression may have become a Western World, twenty-first-century defence against those realities we dread most.

In the end Hamlet muddles through, not gloriously and, at the last, still not altogether in control, but determinedly asking questions and searching for some answers of his own. In Edward Bond's comedy, *The Sea* (1973), the enormity of a young man's drowning is set against the minutiae of daily life in an isolated seaside village. We watch the characters trying to make sense of their lives. Rose, the dead man's fiancée, asks his friend Willy, 'How can you escape from yourself, or what's happened to you, or the future?' Willy replies,

> If you look at life closely it is unbearable. What people suffer, what they do to each other, how they hate themselves, anything good is cut down and trodden on, the innocent and the victims are like dogs digging rats from a hole, or an owl starving to death in a city. It is unbearable but that is where you have to find your strength. Where else is there? ... So you should never turn away. If you do you lose everything. Turn back and look into the fire. Listen to the howl of the flames. The rest is lies. (p.148).

It's in this disillusionment that Willy suggests a way forward, understanding that it's our *illusions* which really kill us when they no longer contain or make sense of our experience. Then we break down.

I don't think it matters that we don't know things. Nor do we need be scared to admit as much to young people, if that allows them not to know things as well rather than go on pretending they do until something destroys their illusion. We're actually all in it together. Provided we're all allowed to ask the same fundamental questions we have an equal opportunity of each finding our own way of negotiating the situation. Willy suggests that after existential dread may come a kind of faith: not the faith of blind obedience to one big idea but an open-mindedness, not propped up or defended against with illusions, but aware, alive, kicking.

CHAPTER 6

What's Good For You
Helping Young People Evaluate Feelings

> Silver tongues are speaking long and tired into the night
> I must be myself and I'll do alright

Famous for her singing with Fairport Convention before deciding to go solo, Sandy Denny was clearly sceptical about the advice of the silver tongues in her song, 'What is True?' (1973). Her tragically brief life illustrates how difficult it became simply to 'be herself' without the support of alcohol and other drugs (Irvin 1998).

Young people are bombarded with similarly well-meaning exhortations – 'Be true to yourself! Do what feels right! Trust your heart! Follow your instincts! Listen to your feelings!' This all sounds straightforward, but the hard bit is knowing what any of it means in practice. When parents and other adults say, 'You don't know what's good for you!' they're probably right. What is 'good', anyway? What does 'good' feel like inside and how's anyone supposed to know? What if something feels 'good' at the time but later turns out to be destructive?

Difficult though it may be, I think it's important to help young people make sense of this. As it stands, they're never short of advice and are always being told what's good for them. But all that advice and reasoning makes little difference. If reason were powerful young people wouldn't smoke or use other dangerous drugs, nor would they take risks with sex, cars and crime. Their lifestyles would be extremely healthy and they'd be forever opening savings accounts. Clearly, something more than reason prevails.

Counselling is one way for young people gradually to make sense of their experience and develop an *emotional intelligence* to meet the demands of so many new situations. I want to illustrate different ways in which some of the processes of counselling might actually do this.

Sarah's thirteen. She wishes she could see more of her Dad, who's remarried and sometimes doesn't even turn up to collect her as arranged on Saturdays. 'After I got into trouble with the police my Dad heard about it and he took me and my little brother out but he said we looked like tramps. I thought, well if you looked after us properly we wouldn't look like tramps! Anyway he bought me some clothes and bought my brother a computer game and that was it, but what I was hoping was that he'd take me out to dinner on my own and we could talk about it properly.'

Already Sarah appears to know that what's good for her is internal rather than external. It's time with her Dad she wants, not clothes to cover over the neglect she feels and which he possibly senses. But how does Sarah know this?

One answer is that some people search for a contentment and safety they knew as babies. Sarah's father left when she was five. Perhaps, despite all the rows, the violence and her father's absences during those first five years, Sarah internalised some sense of good fathering. However brief the experience, it may have lodged somewhere in her. Or perhaps people experience good fathering from all sorts of other father-figures in their lives anyway, and this is just as valuable as from an original father. Either way, Sarah's faith in her father's capacity to care for her is touching, given all that's happened to her. Despite his continual cruelties, his failure even to visit when she was in hospital recently, she still holds out the hope that he can be the dad she needs.

Adults talk scathingly about young people knowing the price of everything and the value of nothing. It seems that Sarah knows only too well the value of a relationship with her father but is unsure what price she ought to pay for that relationship. It's easy to imagine her in ten years' time, living with a violent, unreliable partner, still holding out for those few tantalising moments of tenderness.

I suggest the idea of two dads: a dad who can be there for her and a dad who can't. She agrees, yes, that's what it's like. We position two chairs in the room. At my suggestion she sits in the first chair and becomes the dad who *can* be there for her. I ask him about himself and his relationship with his daughter. 'It's true,' he says, 'I do love her but I can't show her and I know I keep letting her down. I do want to be there for you,' he adds, addressing Sarah's chair.

I move Sarah back to being herself in her own chair. She looks at the now empty chair representing this dad. 'I love you too,' she says. 'I don't ever want to lose you.'

We turn to the other chair and Sarah sits in it, becoming the dad who can't cope. 'Why do you forget your meetings with Sarah?' I ask him.

'I don't know,' she answers as this dad. 'Sarah's still only a kid so I don't reckon it matters so much. When I'm with my mates in the pub I just forget about her!'

Sarah returns to her own chair. I ask what she needs to say to this dad. 'I've had enough of you!' she says. 'You're a bastard. I don't want to see you any more!'

By externalising what's been for so long an internal dynamic, Sarah becomes clearer about what she does and doesn't need. Before, the dads were mixed up. Now she looks from chair to chair, making sense of them. We talk about how her 'good' dad exists but isn't around much, whereas her 'bad' dad seems to be around so much of the time. We talk about whether she might keep and treasure one dad and stop waiting so painfully for the other to change.

These dads are also parts of Sarah herself projected into the chairs: the part of her that can love herself and the angry, destructive part that can't. Both parts are real, coexisting in her: a kind, loving person as well as an unkind, hating person. In the long run Sarah's learning will be about how to contain both parts of herself and find an equilibrium without constantly and unsuccessfully seeking to annihilate one part or the other. She's both. And her Dad is the dad she's been given: good and bad, saint and sinner, adequate and inadequate just like her.

But part of what makes it more possible for her to accept the limitations of her inadequate dad is to do with her experience of me. I imagine that in our sessions Sarah experiences a man who listens patiently, who's reliable, who doesn't mind her anger and who can take some responsibility with her for shaping the counselling work. All these are qualities she might ascribe to her adequate, good dad but which she *experiences* each week in her sessions with me. The more she experiences them and experiences herself as worthy of them, the more she can let go of her painfully inadequate dad and treasure instead the adequate dad who exists in her heart and who *can* be there for her.

Young people may take all sorts of insights away from counselling, but what they usually value most is simply their relationship with the counsellor. 'She was there for me. She listened and seemed to understand. She didn't think I was stupid.' For some, an experience of safety, consistency, trust and acceptance may be their first experience of these qualities. It may be a revelation. 'I'd never been taken seriously before! He didn't seem fazed! I felt like he was bothered!' This can go some way towards balancing previously hurtful, unsafe experiences with adults and can give young people a broader emotional repertoire with which to respond to life's dilemmas, because to some extent we can only give other people what we ourselves have been given, we can only deal with situations the way other people have dealt with us.

On counselling skills courses students are taught about 're-flecting back', which at its most simplistic means listening to what the client says and repeating it back, usually in a condensed form. The client then confirms what the listener's said: 'Yes, that's right,' or amends it, 'Well, what I really mean is ...' But the underlying process is about trying to clarify the client's feelings, using the listener as a mirror to reflect them back in this way. When an angry teacher or stern judge says, 'I want you to reflect on your actions!', he or she means 'I want you to find some per-spective, I want you to step outside and look at yourself.' Unfor-tunately in schools and courts this usually implies 'And I'm going to tell you what you *should* be seeing when you *do* look at yourself!'

The idea of reflecting *for oneself* is central to the process of counselling. As babies we imitate and are imitated by the face gazing down at us. From that face, mirror-like, we learn how our expression looks: what angry and what happy look like. And we learn further discriminations between good and bad feelings (Winnicott 1971) as we copy and are copied by the face. There's a mutuality: mother learns to understand our expressions and noises while we learn to understand hers. But as we grow and begin to separate from mother we encounter a bewildering range of other expressions, noises, faces and behaviours in the world which we have to make sense of. Our own repertoire, our *learning*, increases accordingly but we have to work it out for ourselves. So counselling offers young people a safe face to return to from adolescent travels, a face in front of which to digest and reflect on so much complicated experience.

One of the hardest things a young person has to learn is to distinguish between 'what's me' and 'what's not me'. In deciding whether or not to continue with her boyfriend Zakia finds it hard to distinguish between what's good for her and what's good for him. Like many young people she persists with a seemingly inappropriate partner, believing that her well-being and her partner's are inseparable. So I work with her on other, earlier, more important separations in her life which she hasn't quite made and which underlie her present confusion. It appears that she can't let go of the sisterly role she's always played for her mother or the self-sacrificing, nursing role she's come to play for her depressed father. In counselling Zakia rages against her mother, who 'doesn't have a real life for herself.' I ask whether Zakia sometimes feels like this about herself. She laughs, recognising and accepting the interpretation. I ask whether she's taken into herself all her mother's frustration with men who can't seem to help themselves. She thinks carefully ...

This can be slow work, using the mirror of counselling to tease out the projected and introjected parts of ourselves and other people in order to get some sense of who we are and how we do feel. Zoe comes to see me at the suggestion of her teacher. I've been told that terrible things have been happening recently in her life and her teacher's idea is that Zoe will benefit from talking about these things. She sits sideways on her chair, facing the door, half turned away from me. I ask her to tell me a little about herself. She tells me some brief facts. There's been a difficulty at home recently, she notes, but that's all sorted out now.

I get the message. Now may be far too soon in her life for Zoe to look back and make sense of what's happened. She's evolved a way of coping which is working for her at the moment. But I think her reluctance to engage with me is also about talking as an activity. How can *talking* ever help? How can mere *words* ever be consoling? How can a *relationship* ever feel supportive? Because I'm not able to offer her anything tangible, Zoe therefore doesn't believe I have anything to offer her at all, and she isn't going to stick around to find out. Politely, she leaves.

Other young people come to counselling and want to spew everything out as soon as they enter the room. I'm supposed to be an emotional toilet. Then they won't return for a second appointment because their brief relationship with me was quite ungrounded in reality. Because it was so one-sided it was barely a relationship at all. So I try to interrupt and explain that it's sensible to keep back certain things until they're sure they can trust me better. They can go slowly instead, digesting the experience. That way, our relationship is more likely to be worth something in the long run.

But for many young people this is a weird idea. They expect gratification to be instant, to be fast like eating or sex, and, because relationships are difficult, they expect counselling to provide immediate answers. They struggle, wondering how on earth something slow can ever be satisfying, how something gradual can ever be good. It may well be that their earliest experiences of learning/feeding from the face/breast were neither slow nor gradual but rushed and begrudging. There may have been no time to digest and relish that first relationship, to *reflect*, and consequently they now have no time for any comparable relationship. They need to know. There's an old story about two mothers who go before the king with a baby, arguing over which of them is the mother. The king says that, as they can't agree, he'll cut the baby in half and they can each have half. 'No!' says one woman. 'Rather than that, let her have my baby!' The king gives the baby to this same woman who, through her selflessness, has proved she must be the baby's mother.

Young people search for emotional proof. Not finding it, they resort to behaviour such as overdoses, drunkenness and running away because not knowing, not having tangible proof of love, self-worth, security, is just too much to bear. To prove the sincerity of his music, Richie James of the Manic Street Preachers famously carved '4 REAL' into his forearm in large, bloody cuts. This has become especially fascinating for young people since, leaving his car near the Severn Bridge one day in 1995, James disappeared.

Parents are also anxious to prove their love. Each year, before Christmas, I listen to long lists of presents young people are expecting and will undoubtedly get from their parents. From her Mum and Step-dad Ellie expects a video player to go with her TV, plus clothes, CDs and her school trip to France paid for.

From her Dad she'll get a bike (though she doesn't really want one), new trainers, several videos and money. Ellie gets these presents. They will distract her for a few weeks until the illusion wears off and she and I return, sometime in the New Year, to her continuing anxiety about her real worth.

Like Ellie, many young people surround themselves with possessions so as to believe they're worth something, not because they're foolish but because they've never felt valuable in any other way. John, though hopelessly in debt, can't bear to give back his hire-purchase car. It represents his sense of achievement in the world, his potency, his attractiveness. When he sits in the car he feels good, he says, and yet the HP payments are wrecking his life. He reckons that without this car he'll feel like a failure. In counselling we go back to the beginning, when John first started to believe (and people probably started to tell him) he was no good at things. His father left, he says, when he was nine. His mother then had a string of boyfriends, none of whom stayed long, and most of whom mistreated her. As her only child, John tried to comfort his mother, to intervene when men appeared, but he could do nothing. When one man hit her she told John not to worry, to go back to his bedroom and sleep. He 'sort of gave up', he says, and never felt good about his mother after that.

I think (but don't say) that our work together will involve thinking through this time in his life so that John can find ways to forgive his nine-year-old self for not having been a grown man capable of standing up to other grown men; for having been his mother's son, not her husband. If John can come to see himself less in terms of external, tangible success or failure – what he can and can't *do* – but rather as a person, full of feeling, who at the age of nine was put in an impossible situation, he may come to rely less on external symbols to prop up his poor internal sense of self-worth and begin to develop an alternative way of evaluating himself and his life.

I have a friend I play cricket with who, whenever he makes a mistake, berates himself in the third person: 'Oh! David!' What's interesting is the way he instinctively steps out of himself in observing his mistake. The mirror in his head is critical, never praising but seizing instantly on his blunders. Many young people have similar mirrors, voices in their heads, always telling them when they've done something *bad*. They don't have an equally well developed mirror to compensate, telling them when they've done something well.

Counsellors could challenge these critical voices by heaping dollops of praise and admiration on to their clients. This would make counsellors very popular for five minutes and then hugely disappointing once the effect wore off. Rather more helpful is for a counsellor to be warm but to stay reasonably opaque and non-judgemental so that young people can begin to discover and develop their own sense of a mirror, helping them to tell good from bad.

Most young people do already have a positive, strong part of themselves tucked away from some earlier relationship or experience, but it requires the counsellor to help find that part and reintroduce it to him or her. When someone's describing a situation in which they feel particularly helpless or defeated, I might ask, 'Who would understand what you're feeling?' or 'Who in your life could stick up for you? Who could speak for you in this situation? Who would know what to do?' If they think back far enough or delve into their imaginary worlds, most young people can find another person, be it a relative, friend or hero, who can answer the call. What matters is that the character, real or imaginary, has been internalised as 'good'. So it might be a grandmother who was always kind, a childhood friend who was always doing brave things, a TV detective who always stuck up for underdogs … I ask what that character would say now or, better still, I ask the young person to sit in another chair and 'become' the character so that I can ask that character myself. That character's supportive words mirror back to the young person what he or she already knows, possibly from the distant past, but has blocked or lost touch with. We can hear in 'others' what we can't always hear in ourselves. By reintegrating that consoling or supportive voice in this way a young person can feel better equipped to deal with what would otherwise seem like a hopeless situation.

Louise's situation seems hopeless to her teachers. She's been missing a lot of school recently. She comes into the counselling room and tells me she's fine. She's been getting stoned with friends in a nearby town which has been fun, she says, but in her last year of school she hasn't been getting any homework done. 'I have loads of good times,' she complains, 'but not enough *right* times!' The times she does have in school are fraught: she quarrels constantly with teachers and peers. Bion (1961) describes how anxious groups resort to 'fight or flight' as a means of self-preservation. Louise, for her part, seems either to be fighting school or in flight from it. Simply to stay and take part ordinarily is proving too difficult.

It emerges that her parents use a similar tactic. At home they either fight each other or escape from each other: one to endless bodybuilding, the other to evening classes. My job initially will be to help Louise think about the anxiety of staying in school and how she might contain it differently. I imagine school feels like her family: a place where no one notices, where too much is expected of her, where she feels let down by adults. Any work about containing this anxiety will be mirrored in her relationship with me. As a counselling appointment approaches and her anxiety mounts, will she run away, either by forgetting the appointment or by staying away from school altogether? Or will she dare to come through the door, half-expecting to be let down? If she does come through the door and *isn't* let down she may dare to invest further in her relationship with me and then potentially in relationships with other adults. Eventually she may invest again in her relationship with her own hurt self.

As she talks, several times she finishes stories with 'I just can't see the point!' I ask her whether there is a point? She looks confused. 'What if there isn't a point? Or what if nobody really knows what the point is but they all pretend they do?'

Something clicks. She recognises the thought as her own and we explore it for the rest of the session. I wrote in the last chapter about the importance of giving young people permission to think these thoughts, not least because they then don't have to feel so anxious, or in Louise's case, angry about somehow never seeing The Point. The adult world tells her about a future she can plan for, but Louise already knows from painful experience that things don't go to plan; in fact, the more you plan the more you get disappointed. So at the moment 'good times' seem better than 'right times'. She abandons herself to chance and avoids responsibility. But even that's hard. Young people are instinctive planners, forever planning sleepovers, clothes to wear, weekends, holidays, love affairs ... Louise says she wants to have her own family one day.

There are lots of issues in her life and this is only a start, the making of a relationship in counselling which can sustain her through the next months. Louise will survive, though, because she already discriminates between 'good times' and 'right times'. She may not like it, but she knows what's best for her.

Sometimes the job of a counsellor is to provide the right *conditions* within which young people will then resolve things for themselves, in much the same way as a gardener first prepares the soil, making sure there's plenty of light and water: then the plant does its own growing.

Josh comes into my counselling room. We worked together a year ago when he was having trouble starting school. Now it's the beginning of his second year. I ask how things are going. 'I keep losing friends!' he says immediately. He tells me about his childhood best friend, Matthew, and his new friends in school, of whom Ricky is the one he likes to spend time with. Ricky's exciting. 'He's one of the cool lads,' Josh says, 'and he's fun to be around.' I ask about Matthew. Josh squirms. 'Matthew was my best mate,' he says, 'and he still is, in a way. He's a really *safe* sort of friend.' Matthew's evidently upset because Josh is spending less time with him. Ricky and the cool lads think Matthew's seriously uncool. I see Josh's dilemma. And as our session draws to a close he adds, almost as an afterthought, 'I want to talk about my girlfriend as well. I feel passionate about her!'

It seems that three parts of Josh are jostling for attention: the child ('safe'), the teenager ('cool') and the adult ('passionate'). All are real, all are powerful, but they're calling out to him from different parts of the developmental playground.

When we meet for our second session, his grandfather's just died. 'He was my *best* friend,' Josh explains. 'He was like me.' He shows me a photo of his grandfather and goes on to tell me about several other relatives with life-threatening illnesses. I remind him of his phrase, 'I keep losing friends', but he makes nothing of the connection. We talk instead of how he might hold inside what was important about his grandfather; how he might keep memories, like photos, safe.

When we meet for our third session he tells me about his grandfather's burial. His parents wouldn't let Josh attend the funeral, presumably because in their eyes he remains a child, but they did allow him to attend the burial. He worried about crying, he says, and 'being strong'. He tells me how everyone in the family is going to have to look after Nan now that she's on her own. We talk again about how much he's losing and how much he's able to keep of what his grandfather meant to him. I think to myself about Josh's childhood and Matthew, and whether his grandfather's death will prove to be the event Josh has needed to move him on to a position where he can keep all that Matthew meant but feel less guilty about moving on and leaving him behind.

In our fourth session he talks more about his concerns for Nan. After a while I ask how things are with Matthew and Ricky. 'Oh, that's okay now,' he says. 'I haven't been seeing much of either of them.' The session draws to a close. He hesitates before telling me calmly that he doesn't need to come any more. I nod in agreement. My job has been to contain and understand his initial anxiety about friends. While I've kept those anxieties safe in the counselling room, an external event in Josh's life has decisively moved him on from the part of the playground where he'd got stuck.

Perhaps the most obvious way young people evaluate their experience is by comparison with others. When everyone else responds to a situation in a particular way we're inclined to copy. But being like everyone else doesn't always feel right for the individual, and so working with young people *in groups* is a vital way of helping them explore difference and similarity.

Typically, when boys start a group they see only difference. Perhaps because of homosexual anxiety or because of some cultural sense of having to be heroically alone, they struggle at first to find anything they might conceivably have in common. Girls, on the other hand, are inclined to see only sameness. Their tyranny is about having to like the same things and have the same opinions.

I set up structured exercises whereby group members can talk about how they see themselves and each other. As they feel safer, boys dare to admit things in common and girls dare to explore differences. Each person also has a 'portrait': a rudimentary outline of their head and shoulders drawn on paper and stuck to one of the surrounding walls. Towards the end of each session group members are encouraged to write on each other's portraits the *positive* things they've noticed about each person during the session. They must write their comments on the outside of the head, not inside it. And they must only write positive things, I tell them, not because negative things don't exist but because we're already constantly made aware of those aspects of ourselves by other people.

As the weeks go by, the portraits build up. At the last session each person takes his or her own portrait off the wall and has to transfer to the inside of the head all the things people have written which they themselves agree with, adding any other positive things which are also true but which people haven't yet noticed. I ask people to select three things they've now got in their 'heads' and we go round the group with each person saying, as assertively as possible, 'I am ...', then using each of the three descriptions. Everyone takes their portraits away with them.

A portrait like this is essentially a kind of mirror and the experience of being in a group reflects back to members ways in which they're both different from and similar to other people, helping them get some perspective on their own feelings, to 'hold as t'were the mirror up to nature'. We look for ourselves all the time in novels, plays, television soaps, in the characters we identify with. We see ourselves reflected in our surroundings. Typically, we greet each other with the weather: 'Chilly, isn't it?' or 'Warmer today!' Perhaps the weather provides a *frame* within which to begin a conversation: two tentative figures under a light drizzle of uncertainty.

I began a workshop on a residential course for A-level students studying poetry by asking them to think how they would each describe themselves if they were a kind of weather. They shared their thoughts with each other. I asked them what they would be if they were each a specific kind of landscape. Again they shared their thoughts in small groups. I then asked them which animal they would *not* be, which animal they would *like* to be and which animal they would identify themselves with at this moment in their lives.

We turned then to Ted Hughes' poem, 'Ravens' (1979), which describes an adult and a child encountering a landscape where a raven has just been picking at the intestines of a lamb born dead, while other sheep and their lambs munch the grass nearby and the surrounding hills look on. Different students took on the roles of adult, child, dead lamb, raven, mother ewe and hills. Each 'character' spoke in his or her role and there was some dialogue between the protagonists: the raven told of his amoral, mechanical instinct; the mother of the dead lamb laughed it off as just one of those things; the mother of a live lamb said she wasn't bothered as long as her own lamb was safe; the hills said they were powerless; the adult told the child that nature was like this; the child said she didn't understand. Only the dead lamb complained that this wasn't fair, that she couldn't feel 'part of anything' and that she felt sad.

I asked everyone to go to the character they identified most with and share with the others gathered there what it was they identified with. Groups of roughly the same size formed around all the characters except the dead lamb. The dead lamb was left entirely alone.

Foulkes (1975) writes about the group mind: the idea that every group works as a single, composite mind. Different voices will be heard but they'll usually balance one another, just as in one person's head different voices will be contained, balancing and cancelling one another out. I think this group's collective behaviour spoke for each individual. Everyone could identify in some way with all the characters except, apparently, the dead lamb. I think the dead lamb was nevertheless probably the most powerful focus of *everyone's* identification: they *all* knew and dreaded what it might be like to feel abandoned, alone, invisible, unloved, useless, but that part of themselves was too dangerous to acknowledge, too close to the surface and raw, so the group defended absolutely against it. They could see themselves reflected in their surroundings, but only the parts of themselves they could bear to see.

In a long-term group this might result in the persecution of the person representing the 'dead lamb' voice (the weakling, the odd one out). This brief workshop revealed much about this group's discomfort with its own most vulnerable part. Only with careful intervention can a group's confidence develop to the point where people begin to acknowledge such a vulnerable part of themselves, and this is usually only possible once people

have first celebrated those parts of themselves that *can* cope and
do succeed. With these parts safely established (as perhaps this
group was seeking to do), group members can bear to acknowledge more vulnerable, frightened parts of themselves
without having to project them all on to one poor, persecuted
person.

Young people find all sorts of ways to distance themselves
from painful feelings. Levi's Dad isn't allowed near the family
any more after attacking them in the street and at home. Levi
tells me about the computer games he plays at home in which
characters get mutilated and blown to bits. In all these games
Levi seems to be endlessly defending himself from attack on all
sides. Listening, I feel exhausted.

I learn that Levi can scan a photo of his Dad into one game.
The photo is imposed on to the face of a bad character so that
Levi can attack it. This is really good, he says. I ask which character is most like himself. He tells me about one called Lal who
cries a bit but is brave. I ask what Lal needs. 'Friends to stick up
for him,' says Levi. 'He just wants to be left alone.' I imagine my
role in counselling will be as Levi's temporary friend. In counselling he'll be left alone to think and talk in peace, away from
the gunfire and explosions. Counselling will be a field hospital
where Levi can recover and rest.

Because his recent family experience is too difficult to talk
about directly, we talk about it obliquely through the computer
characters. And as our sessions go by Levi begins to describe Lal
differently. Lal is now looking for friends in the game and has
got more skilful, Levi says, at avoiding bullets. He knows when
the bad characters are coming and hides. Once they've gone
away Lal comes out and plays with his friends. As we talk about
the characters, I suggest new perspectives on them, wondering
how they got to be so violent and whether they can also sometimes be kind, gently challenging Levi's initial stance where
every character was trying to attack him and his whole effort
went into defending himself. Gradually we begin to talk about

the real people in his life, including his Dad. Together, we're restoring a sense of what might be good (friends, calm, kindness, play) to set against Levi's already well developed sense of what's bad.

Being numb is an effective way for Levi not to feel feelings. There are reasons, after all, why it's safer *not* to know what we feel. Knowing what we *do* need and *do* feel is dangerous because then we either have to set about satisfying that need or feel its frustration. A hungry baby knows satisfaction depends entirely on another person, usually its mother, which is why the idea of independence sounds absolutely wonderful to most young people, anxious no longer to experience the frustration of needing and not always getting. How wonderful to be independent! And, in the meantime, it's much safer to deny or at least qualify any neediness or strong feeling.

For similar reasons it's also much safer for young people to define themselves in terms of what they're not – 'I'm not gay! I'm not religious! I'm not a wimp!...' – and to define feelings in terms of what they're not – 'I'm not scared! I'm not in love! I'm not angry!'... – because to say, 'Yes, I am really angry!' means that other people are implicitly involved and expressing that anger to them might become necessary. So people say, 'Well, I'm a *bit* angry!' But it's hard to keep powerful feelings under wraps for long and, without the opportunity to talk, young people end up *enacting* what they feel by stealing, damaging, fighting, running away, harming or hurting themselves and others.

Counselling affords young people an opportunity to identify feelings more honestly. The counsellor will keep things confidential and safe and, where there are mixed feelings, will help acknowledge them. Young people can then walk back into the world and make *choices* about whether and how to express feelings to other people, having first been able to clarify just what those feelings are. In this way counselling can be a rehearsal. If young people then, for whatever reason, decide not to express certain feelings in public, they don't have to feel so dishonest or guilty because they've made a considered, honest decision, and if they do decide to speak out, they can make choices about how to do that. Either way, they've 'reflected' on the situation with a counsellor and made their own decision about *what's best.*

Emotional truths are always hard to find because the truth changes. People change. Young people change a lot and often need help in making sense of so many different feelings. Sandy Denny's lovely song ends, still searching for someone to listen and still searching for an elusive truth: a truth she herself appears never to have found:

> The rain beats so impatiently upon the window pane,
> I must close my ears or I'll go insane.
> Can't you be a gentle breeze or silent as a snowfall?
> Won't you even try and listen for the voice behind the wall?
> It cries to you
> Even though it only ever whispers
> Part of what it knows ...
> It's the fingerprint
> Which is never made,
> It's the perfume of a rose.

CHAPTER 7

Brilliant Laughs
Young People's Use of Joking

When I began work in charge of a youth centre I was immediately told a lot of jokes: jokes about black people, gay people, Asian people, Irish people, women.

They watched me. If I laughed I was implicated. If I remained stony-faced I was a killjoy.

The fact that I didn't instantly roll around in hysterics was a disappointment to the white boys telling me the jokes. Their jokes were no doubt meant to bring us together, to establish a friendship, but they were also jokes about perceived outsiders and I was an outsider. Each joke was, in its way, not only a gesture of friendship but also an attack and an expression of the boys' ambivalence: intrigued by me yet wary, hoping this new youth worker would be what they wanted but fearing I wouldn't be what they had in mind at all.

The girls sat by, also watching my response and agreeing with the boys that sexist, racist jokes were only a bit of fun, only a giggle, only a laugh.

Somehow I had to indicate my disapproval or at least my lack of interest in the text (black people are lazy, gay people disgusting, Asian people smelly, Irish people stupid and women only good for sex) while tolerating the subtext which seemed to say, 'Your presence here makes us really anxious. We don't know who you are and we don't know whether you'll like us.' I think an outburst of moral indignation would have missed the point.

I'd have been rejecting their racism, sexism and homophobia, which would have been fine, but I'd also have been rejecting their anxiety, which would have been unkind.

Young people spend a lot of time telling jokes and exaggerated stories. But whereas children enjoy jokes, relishing all sorts of puns and twists and absurdity, I think that as they get older most young people are terrified of jokes. Their joking almost invariably expresses mixed feeling and fear.

I remember the first session I ran with a group of Year 7 boys in a school. One chair-swapping exercise involved everyone first of all introducing himself by saying who his hero or heroine was and why. The first boys spoke about skilful footballers and funny cartoon characters. When it was his turn, Danny announced that his hero was another boy in the group, Mitchell. Delighted with this, I wondered to myself whether Mitchell had had some difficulty in his life which he'd bravely overcome or whether he was simply Danny's best mate and Danny didn't mind other people knowing. So I asked Danny to go on and say why he'd chosen Mitchell.

Danny smiled slowly. 'Because he's a nutter!'

The boys all laughed. Mitchell did a quick 'nutter' impression. He was one of the boys most concerning the teachers, who saw him as already out of control and having a bad effect on the others.

I reminded Danny that we'd made a rule for ourselves about respecting each other and that calling someone a nutter didn't sound very respectful. I asked what it was about Mitchell that Danny really liked.

Like so many adolescent jokes, Danny's was double-edged. He applauded Mitchell ('hero') and attacked him ('nutter'), while the group laughed in recognition because they, too, had mixed feelings about Mitchell: impressed by him (nutters are brave and break the rules) but scared of him (nutters are unpredictable). Danny's joke expressed a collective anxiety.

Freud (1905) distinguishes between 'innocent' jokes and 'tendentious' jokes. Most of the young people I work with *groan* at innocent jokes, the sort that children enjoy. Like the boys in this group they laugh instead at tendentious, hurtful jokes because these are the jokes which tap into and express their anxieties. Freud's suggestion is that a joke works by releasing an idea previously held but repressed in the unconscious. Certainly there are countless examples in literature, film and theatre of the Fool, Clown or Joker as a kind of seer using throwaway jokes to contain oblique truths. In the same way, I think young people use joking to speak the unspeakable because then they can be hostile or critical or truthful about others without being properly challenged: 'Look, it was only meant as a joke! There's no need to take it so seriously! I was joking, okay?'

We went on to do another exercise where they had to imagine things which might be true about one another. As the group focused on another boy, Karl, imagining things about him, Mitchell himself then made a kind of joke. He said, 'I imagine you've got Action Men at home which you've had since you were five and you still play with them!' Again the boys laughed nervously, all probably thinking the same thing, for young people laugh at the very things they themselves worry most about: childhood, stupidity, being alone, being different, cowardice, sex. Jokes become uneasy communications about so many underlying anxieties. Mitchell's joke was clearly about Karl and childhood but I think his 'nutter' persona was also obliquely about childhood. I think being a 'nutter' for these boys was like being a toddler: slightly out of control and therefore embarrassing, unaware of adult social conventions. And the boys in this group *were* toddlers as far as the rest of the school was concerned. They were the smallest, the youngest, the ones taking their first steps in the grown-up world of secondary school, toddling along its bare, chilly corridors.

Because Mitchell's joke wasn't the first of its kind, I decided to intervene. I suggested to the boys that, whether Karl had

Action Men or not, laughing at things other people enjoyed doing wasn't fair because we all enjoyed doing different things and we could all be laughed at. Lawrence, bless him, muttered something like 'We all laugh at things but we all do them ourselves.' I asked him to repeat it so the others could hear.

It became clear that, for all their individual difficulties, this group of boys was desperate for fun, devouring my warm-up exercises and games and always wanting more. It seemed that concentrating on grown-up, secondary school things would be impossible until, like toddlers, they'd *played*. I wondered how much they were missing their primary schools and, to my surprise, they all readily admitted as much. I remembered the way some secondary students (and not just the youngest ones), finishing early at lunchtime on the last day of term, often go down to their old primary schools in the afternoon, not to cause trouble but just to go in and see everyone. It seemed that much of what made this particular group difficult to teach was that, in a way, they hadn't finished playing. Their loss of primary school life hadn't been acknowledged and they were left mourning it angrily, anxiously, messily. Joking or 'mucking about' was the closest they could get to articulating these things.

My task became one of helping them learn to laugh *with* rather than *at* each other. Young people making jokes hardly ever feel safe enough to laugh at themselves. Instead, they make endless jokes against other people. So this group of boys had some way to go. But my experience is that young people do become less inclined to laugh hurtfully at each other – with all the potentially damaging consequences of that – the more they can begin to accept themselves with their *own* fallibilities, differences and needs.

It's easy for adults to underestimate the discomfort of young people getting used to new regimes and expectations, particularly when we've been through it ourselves and don't want to be reminded. The transition of adolescence is uncomfortable because it reminds us at some level of our first transitions as babies and children. Bowlby (1973) describes the urgency of a child's search for safe attachment and the way in which any subsequent loss of that attachment to a parent, sibling or, indeed, to a special teacher arouses anger and anxiety in the child. Developing Freud's notion that we repress and then unconsciously express through jokes the discomfort of such early experience, Phillips (1993) concludes, 'Jokes link us to our losses' (p.91). I think that for many of the boys in Mitchell's group this was the case. Through joking they expressed some of the anger and anxiety they felt about the transition from childhood to adulthood, primary school to secondary school.

However, for Mitchell's group secondary school wasn't just frightening. It was exciting as well. The boys talked enthusiastically of cars, horror films, money, hairstyles: all the essentials of young male culture. And, like comic strips, when they talked they exaggerated. Countless stories young people tell are sharpened up with the spice of exaggeration and not a little swearing. I think the reason for this is that exaggeration clarifies and simplifies experience. It makes things either good or bad, 'totally brilliant' or 'completely crap'. It saves life from the worst possible fate, the unforgivable crime of being boring. 'Boring', of course, is neither good nor bad, fast nor slow, but a mixture, and mixtures (mixed feelings) are dreadfully hard to get used to.

So the alternative to being boring is 'having a laugh'. On Monday mornings older students sit around in dull registration sessions, reminding themselves that at least on Saturday night they had a bit of a laugh, a good laugh, a right laugh, a brilliant laugh! Their Saturday night gets ever more brilliant as the day drags on. Eventually it rises to a higher plain. Saturday night was … crazy! It was completely mad!

I think there's a connection between things being 'crazy' or 'mad' and Mitchell in my boys' group being a 'nutter'. What happened on Saturday night was that the people involved met up and played. They probably got drunk in order to do this, but play is essentially what they did. They said silly things, unsayable things, rude things. They fell over. They giggled. They danced. They did all the things the much younger boys in Mitchell's group also longed to do. Through joking and laughter they were able to express and, to some extent, enjoy again the forbidden experience of childhood, stumbling through a nervous town centre, laughing at people, frightening them and apologising.

Much of what's fun about this is the relief that comes from sharing the joke with others, from 'getting it' in the first place and therefore being part of the gang. Meltzer (1973) identifies a 'flight-to-the-group' phenomenon whereby the adolescent, unable to manage the complexity of his or her own unreliable, changing state, externalises it into the various members of the gang. The gang becomes a chaotic expression of the adolescent. He or she can then go round with it, hang out with it, *play with it*, without feeling responsible for its many facets but nevertheless feeling simplified and contained by it.

Friends express many of their 'gang' credentials through joking. In-jokes are conspiratorial and intimate. They last longer. And reciting catch-phrases or sketches from television comedies, everyone racing together towards the punchline, is another gleefully shared experience, another way of demonstrating that I'm not alone, I'm not stupid, I'm not a child, I'm not different, I'm not afraid and I do understand all about sex.

Umpteen comedians have described learning to joke as young people in order to survive bullying and protect themselves. Peter Cook, for example, seems to have repaired the damage of many childhood abandonments and survived the cruelty of his boarding school by discovering jokes. As a popular joker he was then able to gain some of the acceptance and attachment he'd missed out on as a child (Thompson 1997). I think joking can be another way of fighting. Indeed fighting between young people is often what happens when joking fails. Wandering around school at lunchtime, I come across a big boy typically holding a small boy in a headlock. They grin anxiously. This isn't a fight yet, but it's a situation (a 'play-fight' or 'joke-fight') that will lead to a fight if the big boy squeezes too hard or the small boy struggles too much. I immediately tell the small boy to stop bullying the big boy.

They stop, confused. The big boy laughs, recognising the ludicrousness of my request, and lets go. His status is maintained. The small boy is about to protest his innocence when he realises that this is a joke. He joins in, 'Yeah, I'd better stop now. I'm getting bored of bullying him!' The big boy pretends to be scared and the small boy walks off quickly.

Alternatively, we're at the ice rink. Two girls tell me they're going to take Paul, who can barely skate, out into the middle of the rink and leave him there. 'Only for a joke!' they insist, as if this will somehow make Paul feel fine about the whole thing. Clearly the sight of a boy on his own, clinging to the sides of the rink, has provoked something both tender and sadistic in the girls which they invite me to disentangle. I tell them they mustn't do it and they skate off happily enough.

Joking happens in counselling, too, and can sometimes be cathartic. Suzanne, who's eighteen, tells me how difficult it is when people ask what her small daughter would like for Christmas. Suzanne doesn't know what to say. She's scared of sounding greedy because her parents always accused her of that, so Suzanne has learnt to survive, apparently needing nothing.

I suggest that it must be even harder when people ask her what she herself would like for Christmas.

'It is!' she confirms. 'I don't like to say I want anything!'

'A nice handkerchief!' I say.

She laughs a little and sighs, breathing out, letting go of some small knot of resentment and hurt recognised between us through the joke.

But jokes can be collusive as well. Lauren is an intelligent and funny fifteen-year-old. She talks with adult knowingness of how the world *really* is, making fun of her parents' transparent behaviour. But the way her ironic façade has become so entrenched makes it hard to help her.

As she gets up to leave the counselling room, she comments on my *Romeo and Juliet* film poster. 'I used to really like that film!' she says. 'But I think it was only because I fancied Romeo!'

'Yes,' I reply, 'I guess that was Juliet's problem!'

She goes out with a laugh and I curse myself. Another adult has now colluded with all that smart, joky, defensive stuff, and the next time we meet it'll be even harder to help Lauren think about the parts of herself she's so intent on avoiding.

At the counselling and information service where I worked there was a homemade card from a boy who'd used the service. He'd drawn a picture of a dog with sunglasses, a spiky collar and a bruise on its face. He'd written, 'Thank you for the help'. The dog held out its paw in a friendly way, wearing a green boxing glove.

CHAPTER 8

Walking Slowly

Containing Anxiety in Work with Young People

In her famous study of nurses, Isabel Menzies Lyth (1988) describes the impact of caring for sick people and of being constantly surrounded by suffering and death. Such work, she argues, arouses strong and mixed feelings in frontline staff: feelings of pity, compassion, love, guilt, anxiety, hatred, resentment, envy. Nurses defend themselves against being overwhelmed by such feelings in a variety of ways: they ritualise their work, they make decisions mechanically or not at all, they avoid change, they structure the work so as to avoid becoming attached to particular patients and, in the meantime, idealise themselves and the job they do.

It's important to think about the effect of the job on those who work all the time with young people. Unlike nurses, they're not surrounded by suffering and death but are nevertheless immersed each day in powerful feelings of dependence, love, resentment, guilt, hatred, anger, jealousy, powerlessness, chaos. These feelings come at them constantly from the young people they work with, but also from within themselves. How they contain and manage such feelings is crucial to their effectiveness in the job and crucial to the way young people, in turn, learn to contain and manage difficult feelings.

Not long ago, I was in a staffroom as the bell went for the end of the school day. Three teachers came in and sat down, ignoring me. They talked about the lessons they'd just come from and, in particular, about their most disruptive students who'd apparently got through the last lessons without incident, much to the relief of the three teachers. They began to talk about one particular student's mother who was evidently a professional counsellor but who, they agreed, didn't even know how to look after her own children. Then suddenly the conversation changed tack. In detail they described what and where they were going to eat that evening.

I had to go, but I was left wondering ... Their first need, it seemed, had been to acknowledge the anxiety they'd each felt about their disruptive students and how relieved they were that it was all over for another day. I wondered whether their abiding feelings of inadequacy as teachers, expected to manage the competing demands of so many young people, were then projected on to the counsellor of whom a lot was also expected and whose failure to live up to expectation they so derided. Having shared and projected their anxieties in these ways, they were then able to express their own need for the anticipated feeding, not unlike the looking-after which they'd just been providing for the students.

People find all sorts of ways like these of projecting their anxieties on to other people and into various activities. I managed a part-time youth worker who doubled as the youth centre's cleaner. As a cleaner he was excellent: the building smelt of polish and the darkest corners were spotlessly clean. But in the evenings, as a youth worker, he was quite happy to let young people drop cigarette ends, sweet papers and Coke cans anywhere, treating it almost as an infringement of civil liberties when I suggested we might order more bins, toughen up on litter and move towards a no-smoking policy. I think his cleaning served as a defence against his anxiety about youth work. If he was having a hard enough time cleaning up so much mess day after day, then no one could complain he wasn't effective as a youth worker in managing young people's distress.

After all, he was dealing with their physical messes even if he couldn't deal with their emotional ones.

Alice expressed her anxiety differently. She was a student counsellor who was extremely anxious about her A-levels. As the exams approached, Alice was to be found week after week playing Jenga with younger students: the game where each player carefully removes one brick at a time from the bottom of the tower, piling them on top until eventually there's one brick too many and the whole tower collapses. The game seemed to encapsulate Alice's anxiety that all her careful revision would come to nothing, that something would eventually undermine all her hard work. She looked shocked when I suggested this. Then laughed, recognising herself.

Anxiety is the experience of mixed or painful feelings, and young people express anxiety in all sorts of ways: in arguing, fighting and in bullying, for example. Teachers and other professionals have to deal with all this knowing that, in spite of everything, their work is never enough. A conscientious teacher is forever aware of only reaching part of the class at any one time, of *always* failing some students, however good the intention, however thorough the preparation. In a sense, all teachers are single parents. Alone, they look after thirty children at a time. They must be mother and father. They must represent both the satisfaction and the frustration of students' needs. They must be patient. They must always survive. There's a lot to be anxious about and in the same way that a mother copes with her child's attacks on her by talking to her partner or to other mothers, teachers have to learn to talk to each other in order to contain and make sense of what's happening.

But they rarely do. It's assumed that, after an initial training, teachers and youth workers are experts at human relationships for evermore and will always be able to work things out for themselves. In meetings they talk about everything *but* their own interactions with the young people. These feel too complex and too personal to share unless there's someone holding the reins and making it safe.

Nor do teachers only have to contain the anxieties of *young* people. Other adults ordinarily project a multitude of personal dissatisfactions on to school which have to be coped with by staff. School is a reminder for everyone of separation from our parents, of nervousness, of the people who bullied us, of feeling taken for granted, overlooked, of not being good enough. Most teachers know what it's like to be on the receiving end of someone's misplaced rage at a parents' evening. So when teachers complain of 'overload', officially they mean bureaucratic overload but unofficially they mean emotional overload: they have *loads* of feelings to contain.

Winnicott (1964) writes about the way a baby's crying disturbs its mother because it reminds her of her own repressed need to be held. Because she recognises it, she knows exactly what the baby needs and can provide for it. But on another level, because she recognises it she also competes with the baby, resenting and wishing to crush it. She represses that wish but the conflicting feelings inside make her anxious. Young people aren't babies but, in their transition from child to adult, they also spend a lot of time crying for attention. They want to be little and they want to be big. They want to hug and they want to hurt. They want to be attached and they want to be separate. The power of these and other conflicting feelings is experienced by the professional every day. He or she must contain them, must stay calm, must understand. But what happens when the professional inevitably *shares* these feelings?

Projective identification (Holmes 1992) is the process whereby a person projects a part of him- or herself that he feels uncomfortable about on to someone else. That other person receives the projection and internalises it *because it resonates with his or her own discomfort.* So, for example, a male student winds up a female teacher. The student, who daren't express his own intense anger, appears calm as the teacher gets more and more angry. With some teachers this doesn't work because they're perfectly comfortable with their own anger and irritating students are, for them, easy to manage. But with others it works a treat because the student has discovered a part of the teacher that happens to be bubbling away inside anyway. This teacher's angry about all sorts of things in her life. She, too, is angry with authority figures. She, too, is angry at always being told what to do. Her eventual outburst in class expresses for the student just what he himself can't express.

Many adults are passionate about young people's lives because they still feel passionately about their own youth. They find themselves working with young people for precisely this reason, and as a result they're the recipients of a lot of projective identification from them. Youth workers have to deal with young people's anxieties all the time and never really know when they've helped. When young people move on from youth workers they're often still in transition. So every subsequent arrest, every unplanned pregnancy, every misfortune can seem like a reflection on the youth workers previously employed to support them. The fierce loyalty youth workers feel towards young people is often fuelled not just by empathy but by identification. They're working with people who constantly remind them of their own adolescence. Pincus and Dare (1978) write, 'The repressed drives and wishes of the adult, which the adolescent may be expressing, constitute ... the secret life of the adult' (p. 116). Much as youth workers may care passionately for the young people they work with, their very identification with these young people is what sometimes makes it hard for them to contain their own anxiety and therefore that of the young people themselves.

On an institutional level, a youth service has to contain not only the anxiety of the adolescents it supports but also the anxiety of adults *about* adolescence. I sometimes wonder whether local authorities cut funding to youth services as a way of punishing young people for being so difficult. When an adolescent has just stolen your car or sworn at you in the street it's hard to believe that this person might need more support rather than less. I think there's usually a connection between how adults feel about their local youth service and how they feel about their own adolescence. For many adults the chaos of adolescence is something to be forgotten and young people are too much of a reminder. The perennial suggestion that young people just need somewhere to go is perfectly sensible in one way, because many of them do need somewhere safe to go, but it may also be an expression of what adults would like to do with their own adolescence or continuing adolescent feelings: round them up and get them into a building with two or three people employed to keep them inside and out of sight for as long as possible.

As it gets older, a child gradually loses its simplicities, its sureties, its wonderful fairy godparents. Bowlby (1973) describes the overwhelming sense of loss and the anger it comes to feel as a consequence. That anger can't always be expressed to an actual parent for fear of losing the parent altogether, so it has to find some other outlet. This is where teachers and youth workers come in. They're on the receiving end. They're paid money not to run away or give up, so they're much safer figures to be angry with. The trouble is that, just as the baby's crying reminds the mother of her own repressed need, young people's behaviour (needing, needing, needing) reminds the teacher or youth worker of his or her own unresolved adolescent feelings. The teacher's own anxiety then either spills out immediately, expressed as extreme vindictiveness or extreme tenderness towards the student, or gets saved for the office or staffroom where some unsuspecting senior colleague encounters an enraged teacher, behaving just like an adolescent: needing immediate reassurance, immediate praise, needing always to be right. Alternatively, the teacher's anxiety is contained in some other, more satisfactory way which allows the teacher routinely to examine and reflect on his or her own interactions.

I used to supervise a counsellor who, for a while, always managed to make me feel quite useless. I never seemed to understand the particular client she kept talking about, or be of any help. Discussing it with my own supervisor I began to realise that the counsellor was getting me to feel her own sense of uselessness. Every fortnight she arrived, dumped it on me and left. Only once I realised what was happening could I begin to help.

As she paused, I said, 'I don't know what to say, Michelle. I feel quite useless.'

'So do I!'

Something shifted. Together, we saw that this was just what her client was doing to her: getting her to feel his uselessness so that once a week in counselling he could effectively relieve himself. Nothing would be resolved until he acknowledged his own feeling of uselessness and, with the counsellor's help, began to address it.

Feelings get passed along the line in this way from client to counsellor to supervisor, from student to teacher to headteacher. Unless someone contains the anxiety of the professionals, flooded as they are with conflicting feelings, the professionals themselves can't do it for young people. The buck has to stop somewhere. When the teacher starts ranting or the youth worker starts blaming or the counsellor despairs, a manager has to be calm, to listen, to accept. To respond in equal measure isn't supportive, may well be vindictive, and simply leaves the worker feeling unsafe. If the person at the top can't contain his or her anxiety then the whole organisation suffers. People stop listening to one another and their official professional views merely reflect how they happen to be feeling inside. Like young people, adults need to believe that someone somewhere knows what's happening and why it's happening, has seen it all before and is coping. Otherwise the world seems just too dangerous. I think this is a reasonable expectation and different from the dream of an omniscient, omnipotent leader who'll always make everything all right. Some schools, like some children, invest in that dream, surrounding the boss with trappings to make him or her appear even more fantastic: an academic gown, perhaps, an inaccessible office or a culture of deference. When he or she fails to live up to such unreal expectations, everyone anxiously looks for more immediate solutions.

Punishing the students can seem like one solution. Most schools have someone (usually a man) in charge of organising and running detentions. Teachers always have particularly strong feelings about this person because he has a unique insight into their shortcomings. Because of detentions he gets to know all about the homework not done, the rows, the swearing. He *only* gets to know about the unsuccessful parts of their work. So they defend against the detention teacher with pretended care- lessness – 'He doesn't know what goes on! It's no skin off my nose what he thinks about me! He probably likes doing detentions! Anyway, none of my kids can stand him!' Never- theless, they readily use the detention system and would hate to see school detentions abolished because they need to believe that a mechanism exists which can always back them up, run by someone who can always manage the most difficult students. Teachers need the detention teacher but despise him because they despise the part of themselves that needs him, the part of themselves that remains vulnerable and sometimes needs support. If they were able to acknowledge that part more openly they could then think much more creatively about how to *share* responsibility for managing difficult behaviour.

Detentions are sometimes given by way of retaliation when a teacher is feeling particularly punished or is feeling attacked; so hearing that, despite all our mistakes and shortcomings, we're actually doing okay makes us much less anxious and less inclined to retaliate. Hearing that we've done something really well makes us inclined to do it again. Yet amongst teachers and youth workers there's often a distinct shortage of praise. Perhaps this is because young people are such praise junkies. They can't disguise it. Our capacity to give depends partly on what we've been given and, exhausted by the little junkies, we then begrudge having to praise other colleagues, tightening up inside if we feel we're not getting enough praise ourselves. It gnaws away … all those hours of painstaking work behind the scenes that nobody recognises, all that slog taken for granted. In my experience, unsolicited praise causes teachers to melt with pleasure. They beam and spontaneously start praising their students. But who starts that ball rolling? Who praises the headteacher, the service manager, the parent?

If a teacher or youth worker manages to contain a young person's anxiety, somehow putting metaphorical arms around him or her, who, in turn, does that for them? They have their own raw moments. Some complain of 'losing a sense of who I really am'. Many describe having to put on a mask in order to cope with their professional role. In their anxiety to manage so many different demands, they get stuck between their intention to be kind and their reflex to be spiteful.

One of the saddest things in staffrooms is where disillusionment has set in. Older teachers, upset that their best efforts appear to have failed (students *keep* giggling, swearing, forgetting and fighting year after year after year), adopt a cynical mask to deflect the hurt. Younger teachers appear, rushed off their feet and struggling, yet still believing absolutely in the ideals of teaching. The idealism of these younger teachers is too much. It hurts too much to be reminded of one's own original self-confidence, so the older teachers set out to destroy it. Bewildered younger teachers are then caricatured as naive, not confident; with illusions, not ideals. By attacking them, the older teachers expect to feel better, destroying the painfulness of so much hope. When younger teachers get ill because their own defence mechanisms are still inadequate, this is seen in the cynical corner of the staffroom as somehow proof of foolishness. With public displays of uncomplaining commitment, the older teachers trudge off gleefully to cover the lessons. They've survived and the younger ones haven't. Yet they know the awful truth that the younger teachers will still be around and will still be doing things long after they've gone.

I've been privileged to work with some of these older teachers as they've approached retirement. In the privacy of my counselling room they've taken off their masks and I've met idealists, still passionate about young people, still wondering how to make the system better, but *tired* and needing to make sense of so many personal and professional changes. For some it's the first time they've talked about their work like this in thirty-five years, partly because, for whatever reasons, they've always resisted whatever support was available and partly because the possibility of support was always *too* enticing. They imagined they'd never be able to function properly again if they peeped behind the mask.

A stiff-upper-lip culture serves no one. It gets a certain kind of job done, mechanically, but it changes nothing. I'm also able to work with younger teachers who use me to talk through their relationships with particular students or groups of students. We think about their part in these relationships and what the teachers themselves are needing. We think about what the teachers represent for students and how certain students' behaviour might express some underlying need. When people understand why they feel as they do it lessens their anxiety. Professional counsellors meet with a 'supervisor' every week or fortnight to discuss clients the supervisor will never actually meet. Talking in this way, seeing where the counsellor's own feelings are getting muddled up with the client's, the counsellor can make better sense of relationships which have got stuck or which he or she feels anxious about. Such a facility ought to exist for teachers and youth workers. Planning things properly makes a difference, but when we're stuck it's usually because we're stuck with relationships and stuck within ourselves.

But it's hard for a stiff-upper-lip culture to change if the person at the top of the organisation has the stiffest upper lip of all. A system of regular supervision must be endorsed by the boss as promoting professionalism and effectiveness rather than weakness. And it needs to be clear that just because we think hard about our relationships with young people doesn't mean we capitulate to their every whim and can't stubbornly insist on rules when that's necessary.

Whenever people are anxious they suddenly get very interested in rules. They want more rules or they want to change the rules. I used to direct plays with young people and at a certain point, usually as the result of some devious trick like asking each of them how to spell their names in the programme, reality would dawn on the cast that our performances were only three weeks away. A delegation would then always come to see me to say that the whole cast thought the production should be put back at least a fortnight, because then it would be really good whereas in only three weeks' time it would be complete rubbish because no one had even learnt their lines yet. Then I had to insist that our performances would go ahead as planned, however bad they might be, and then not mind being told I was stupid and that the eventual disaster would be entirely my fault!

Sticking to clear rules is an important part of containing young people's anxiety, but as Evans (1998) writes, 'Limit-setting and its testing can be viewed as a "game" between an authority figure and youngsters. The therapist's first concern should not be that he win. The aim is to enable the youngster to become a better games player' (p.182). Rules are therefore never an end in themselves but rather a beginning. Good games players no longer need to be reminded of the rules, but without clearly understood rules the game can't even begin.

When I worked in a youth centre, the most nerve-racking occasions were always at discos on Friday nights. So much could go wrong. A hundred and fifty young people were tired at the end of the week. Some had been drinking. Some roamed around, wishing they could be more popular, looking for a fight or a friend.

The only way to contain the situation was to plan everything meticulously and then, antennae quivering, appear *terribly* relaxed once the evening started. We planned exactly where we'd position ourselves, how we'd communicate throughout the evening and how we'd react to every eventuality, so that when the girls' toilet flooded just as a group of older boys were trying to force their way into the building and the phone rang and the disco lights fused and the tuckshop ran out of change (this actually happened), we'd somehow manage. But to do so, we not only had to plan meticulously, we had also to seem relaxed. And that meant always walking slowly, slowly, talking calmly, calmly, and smiling an awful lot. Frowning made people worry. Hurrying made them think something was up. Shouting excited them. The moment our own anxieties spilled out people would get scared, panic, and then it would be almost impossible to retrieve the situation.

Discos brought in money which made other kinds of youth work possible. But there was always another justification for them. A good disco, properly managed, where everyone had fun at no one else's expense, gave young people an important political experience: that it *was* possible for a large group of people to come together and enjoy themselves without someone inevitably spoiling things. Human beings *could* achieve that much. Good discos were an antidote to recurring school assemblies where the larger group got told off because yet again the smaller group had spoilt something. Unless they have an alternative experience, young people can end up believing that collaboration and respect are impossible dreams and that human destructiveness can never be contained.

The quality of the queue was always a good indicator of what the disco would be like. A good queue (single file, with no pushing or queue-jumping) was an essential start, a statement from the workers about how the disco would be run. A bad queue (a bad start) raised everyone's anxiety.

School receptionists are important for the same reason. All sorts of people arrive in school angry, mystified or upset. An orderly reception area, controlled by calm, clear-headed people, reassures and settles everyone including the teachers who, once they've discovered that their receptionists are so good at containing the world's anxiety, often seize the opportunity to offload their own, either by taking their feelings out on the receptionists or by using them as untrained counsellors. The receptionists complain: this is all very well but *they* need looking after too. If they don't get looked after they resign, or stay and become tyrants. I think the tyrannical receptionist is probably just defending herself, as much as to say, 'Well if you're going to behave like babies, crying and having your tantrums all the time, I'll behave like your mother and simply tell you what to do!'

Without adequate systems of supervision and support, a school can end up reinforcing the very anxieties it struggles to contain. In her study of nurses, Menzies Lyth (1988) describes the way a hospital unwittingly helps nurses evade the anxieties provoked in them by their work with patients. It never lets them settle in one place, underuses them, deprives them of personal satisfaction and, as a system, threatens all the time to break down. The nurses' own ways of defending themselves against the deep anxieties of the job have become *institutionalised*, but the institution has done nothing to allay or modify the original anxiety.

Schools refer to certain students as *anxieties*. I sometimes offer to work with groups of students for a limited period of time and certain schools jump at this. 'Yes,' they say, 'as it happens we *do* have a group we'd like you to work with!' This group usually turns out to be the seven most difficult boys in the year, gathered together (so the story goes) for administrative convenience. I always do the work, and I always regret it. My own anxiety to succeed causes me every time to accept an impossible task: that of containing and resolving the school's seven greatest anxieties, so generously offered. Grouping them together is supposed to make them more manageable. It doesn't, because by segregating them from other students it actually seeks to deny their existence, and like all the best anxieties they become more powerful the more they're denied.

The boys' talk and behaviour in these groups with me focuses directly and indirectly on sexuality, failure, dependence, intimacy, control, parents, the future. I suspect these might very well be the seven greatest anxieties at the heart of the school itself and that until the school finds ways of containing its own anxieties it'll continue to be tormented by these seven spokesmen.

A few years ago, in the school where I worked as the counsellor, a gang of about a dozen boys emerged towards the end of Year 10 (fourteen to fifteen-year-olds). It was hard to see what they had in common except their hostility to other people and their constant use of the word 'queer'. As people went past they'd growl 'Queer!' under their breath or shout it across playgrounds from the safety of the gang. It was impossible to know exactly who'd shouted the word so teachers tried to ignore it. Inevitably, younger boys started to copy the older ones.

Challenged, the gang would protest that the word wasn't meant offensively, that they said it to each other as well and that it was just fun. Only once the phenomenon was discussed at a heads-of-year meeting and the decision was made to confront the boys every time the situation occurred did things improve. I think the boys had tapped into and were expressing a core school anxiety about sexuality. They remained intimidating for as long as the school pretended it wasn't happening and wasn't an issue. When eventually they left school the boys stopped going round together and a few months later the whole staff took part in some Equal Opportunities training which focused explicitly on how homosexuality was talked about in school. For the first time teachers discussed their personal and professional anxieties, and within a couple of months a first student in school identified himself as gay. The roof didn't fall in. No one shouted 'Queer!' The school had simply contained its anxiety, not by ignoring it but by acknowledging it.

Some schools can do this more readily than others. What makes one school become so different from another isn't just the amount of money available to it but the way the psychological needs of the people associated with the school have combined to produce a certain effect. From the architect who designed the buildings, through the various headteachers with their own needs and emphases, to influential teachers, parents, governors, caretakers and others, each person has projected him- or herself on to this communal object. The nature of *any* institution is created in this way. What gives a school or youth centre its particular feel is that children and young people are involved. I think this stimulates the childlike anxiety otherwise kept locked in our adult selves, and we create an institution which represents our best attempts to contain that anxiety.

Visiting a friend's school in Derbyshire, I was struck by how different it looked compared to the modern brick and pre-fab buildings I work in. Most of the school was built a century ago out of Pennine stone. It felt permanent, like some great church built to contain the congregation's anxiety about death. I was left wondering how buildings alone might affect young people. The most difficult students, it turned out, actually avoided these old buildings and hung out near the few Terrapin classrooms down by the playing fields. I know some students always position themselves on the periphery as an expression of how they feel about school and that smoking requires a certain physical distance anyway, but I wondered how much they identified themselves with throwaway Terrapins and felt they belonged there rather than seeing themselves reflected in the permanence, the investment, of Victorian stone. The stone buildings seemed to me safer, more *containing* than the Terrapins. But perhaps through these students' eyes they seemed oppressive. Students all have favourite places where they spend break and lunchtimes; places with which they identify; places where they feel safe. The way classrooms, libraries, corridors and canteens are decorated and looked after affects the way students feel. There's always a connection between the building and the behaviour. Given a scabby building, young people will tend to behave scabbily.

In setting up the counselling and information service where I worked, we put a lot of thought into transforming desolate rooms into rooms which would feel welcoming, warm, interesting and cared for so that when young people came in, sometimes speechless with anxiety, the very first messages they received would be these. We've regularly used training sessions to practise greeting people: what we say, how we say it, where we take people, how we manage to convey solidity as well as warmth. Counsellors unused to working with young people often underestimate the importance of these first interactions on the phone, in the corridor or in a main room. Somehow they must sound friendly but clear, kind but not a pushover: otherwise, young people won't come back.

A counsellor not only has to help young people contain their anxiety but must eventually help them modify it or at least help them discover more appropriate defences against it. For example, Alex keeps cutting himself with a penknife. He's angry with his parents, he says, but it's not their fault. In counselling he begins to verbalise his feelings towards others instead of directing them so fiercely against himself with his knife. Kenny comes for counselling because he's disrupting lessons at school. His teachers say he's always seeking attention. In counselling he gets the attention he so badly needs. The eldest of four, Melinda feels unloved by her parents. In counselling she begins to feed on her relationship with her counsellor, steadily, once a week, rather than continue to cram herself full of indigestible food at home and puke it out. With help, Ali begins to understand connections between his use of drugs and his mother's absence in the early part of his life. And for the first time Gillian is able to tell the story of her childhood, after years of painful shyness.

The counsellor listens, a first witness to the events Gillian remembers.

Teachers, youth workers and counsellors have different working methods. But for young people to feel safe and grow, whoever supports them must contain their own adult anxieties as well as the anxieties young people feel and project into them. Adults can do this by planning thoroughly, by always sticking to clear rules, by acknowledging their own anxieties, by examining them regularly in supervision and by supporting each other with praise for the difficult jobs they do. Walking *slowly*, of course, helps.

CHAPTER 9

Secretest Secrets
Young People Managing Privacy

Kerry complains about Steph: 'I've told her some of my secrets but I'm worried that if we now break friends she'll tell everyone just to get back at me!' Apparently Steph tells her own secrets to absolutely everybody. Kerry and the others are obliged to share some of theirs with Steph as proof of friendship, while Steph offers them all the secrets they could possibly want. Kerry senses danger.

Young people deal in secrets as an emotional currency, a way of measuring intimacy. Having a secret is part of having a best friend: exciting and comforting but also sometimes stifling and burdensome. Kerry says her friends sometimes even tell each other their 'secretest secrets', yet still always end up betraying those secrets. It seems that when they get nervous about friendships they accuse each other of not keeping secrets:

'What I told you was supposed to be a secret!'

'And I didn't tell anyone!'

'So how come the whole world knows?'

'I don't know. I didn't tell anyone!'

'You must have!'

'I didn't!'

'Then who did?'

'I don't know. It could have been ...'

I think young people entrust one another with secrets as a first, dependent stage in a relationship, as a way of capturing and keeping someone who seems wholly attractive. They end up betraying those secrets as the expression of a second, ambivalent stage in the relationship when the other person becomes no longer wholly attractive but possessed of real faults and incompatibilities. *I want you* to tell me your secrets becomes *I don't want you* and your secrets any longer. The hardest thing is for young people to move on to a third stage in the relationship where that disappointment and ambivalence about another person can be tolerated, where secrets no longer need to be begged for and then betrayed but can be shared in a gradual way and looked after as no longer the only indicators of a worthwhile friendship. They can be respected simply as *private* without burning a hole in anyone's emotional pocket.

Kerry feels uncomfortable in her group of friends so long as Steph's pressurising everybody to tell. Yet anti-bullying campaigns also advise everyone to tell, survivors of child abuse are encouraged to tell, and confessional TV shows compete with one another to tell the most. Kerry's not sure.

One of the aims of working in groups with young people like Kerry and Steph is to give them an opportunity to explore and become more confident in managing the relationship between their private and public selves. Early in the lifetime of a group we make some rules for ourselves. We make rules about confidentiality, respect, interrupting, name-calling and so on. We write the rules down on a big piece of paper and put it on the wall. Each week we look at it. We make the rules *explicit*. Adults have usually learnt to interpret *implicit* rules and expectations from observing other people's behaviour, but for young people this isn't so clear and until it's clearer it's hard for them to feel safe. Someone suggests a further rule that we should all be honest. Someone else asks how we'd ever know if we were being honest? A third person says we should *try* to be honest. The rules contain and respect different levels of disclosure. Group norms emerge anyway, somewhere between total disclosure and total inhibition. We usually agree to tell outsiders what we did but not what other people in the group said, and we agree that if anyone's in danger or being hurt then we can't keep that a secret. So there's privacy but also a necessary connectedness with the outside world. It's never as simple as straightforward secrecy.

Secrets, after all, are absolute and young people understand about secrets: a thing is either secret or it's not. But *privacy* is relative: there are degrees of privacy, kinds of privacy, and young people have to learn to manage their own and respect other people's. This is difficult when they experience powerfully conflicting needs: on the one hand to be close, loving and intimate with others but on the other hand to be separate and unassailable, dependent on no one. And there are cultural and social differences: some people are happy talking on trains, some are happy undressing on beaches, some hold hands in public, some say how much money they've got ... Young people have a lot to learn.

So a favourite warm-up exercise involves the whole group standing in a line. They take the hands of the people on either side of them. ('Take the hands' sounds less intimate than 'hold hands'.) The person at one end of the line stands stock still. Without anyone letting go of hands, the person at the *other* end of the line then leads everyone round and round the person standing still, in circles, so that he or she gradually gets tied in by bodies as the circles get tighter. I ask what it's like to be in the middle? 'Good!' they say, or 'Too tight!' I tell the group to stay as they are and I invite the person in the middle to get out, without anyone letting go of anyone else's hands. Much struggling and protesting and unravelling happens. I ask how it feels to be outside again. 'A relief!' they say, or 'Can we do it again? I want to be in the middle!'

Symbolically, the group is trying out different levels of intimacy. To be so close may feel claustrophobic or it may feel very secure. Members of the group can see whether they feel more comfortable in the middle or on the outside or halfway in. I don't think it matters if they make no conscious connection between this exercise and their own relationships. I could say, 'And so you see, this is just like real life!', but that would be water off so many ducks' backs. This *is* real life anyway and young people learn mainly by doing.

Informally, young people are wrestling all the time with the possibilities of closeness and separateness, sameness and difference. It can be a relief to find things in common with others but sometimes it's frightening because a young person can just as easily be persecuted for being too familiar as for being too strange. So another exercise involves the group sitting in a circle. One chair is designated as the Hot Seat and the object of the exercise is to get out of the Hot Seat as quickly as possible. Whoever's sitting there says one true thing about themselves which they imagine makes them different from everyone else in the group: for example, 'I had four pieces of toast this morning', or 'I'm feeling fed up', or 'I've been to Jamaica', or 'My Dad's girlfriend's just had a baby' ... If that applies to anyone else he or she must say so and the person in the Hot Seat must think of something else. If not, then everyone moves round a seat and someone else moves into the Hot Seat. The exercise rewards people for being different, because they no longer have to sit in the Hot Seat. The longer the exercise goes on, the clearer it becomes that everyone has things which make them different and this assuages one major group anxiety. If I suspect someone's cheating, 'Yes! My Dad's girlfriend's just had a baby too!' I can ask that person exactly how old the baby is or where it was born: anything to establish a genuine difference.

Being different and being the same takes some getting used to, just as learning to be intimate while retaining one's own and respecting other people's privacy takes time. When two people in a group are particularly good friends the group has to come to terms with that. Must everyone be equally friendly or is it permissible for people to have different kinds of relationships with one another, to enjoy different levels of intimacy, to be closer to some people than others? Some young people hold back, anxious not to be typecast, while others have to be dissuaded from telling everything about themselves. There's a necessary balance to be struck between not saying too much, yet still contributing and perhaps taking a few calculated risks. One person's healthy concern for their own privacy is different from another's inhibition or shame.

Groups sometimes allocate the role of Doesn't-Say-Anything to someone as a focus for their own ambivalent feelings about the group: how lovely to say nothing, but how cowardly! how intriguing, but how pathetic! My job as leader is to return those projected feelings to their owners and, through carefully structured exercises, support anyone who remains silent through fear. I must also find structures to support others whose fear of the potential intimacy of the group is such that they try to sabotage it.

Young people long for intimacy and are afraid of it. A teacher tells me about a student who's been taking things from her store cupboard when her back's turned. At the end of each lesson he then playfully offers them back to her in front of the class. She says she doesn't know whether to laugh or be angry. We discuss the ambivalence of his communication, wanting the things she has stored in her cupboard and sneaking in to steal them but then, having got them, not wanting them at all and wanting to make her seem foolish. His behaviour might express both a desire to be intimate and get inside her as well as a desire to be separate, rejecting what he finds in her. Like many students he expresses at school what can't so readily be expressed at home. When young people find themselves unable to deal with private, internal conflict they find ways of publicising it. Conflicting feelings about mothers, for example, get enacted away from families where they can be explored more safely. This teacher isn't his mother but she's *like* a mother.

Sensibly, the teacher has tried to talk to him at the end of lessons but, while he seems perfectly relaxed with the rest of the class there, he squirms with embarrassment and can barely speak once he's on his own. It's too intimate. When the teacher made an appointment to see him at the end of the day he simply didn't turn up. So, like thousands of teachers, she's left somehow having to steer a course between firmness and understanding.

Clearly our comfort or discomfort with different kinds of intimacy stems from an experience of earlier relationships and, potentially, from our first relationships with mothers. Suttie (1935) describes a pre-war society where there exists a 'taboo on tenderness'. Children are subject to premature 'psychic weaning' from mothers, he argues; they're separated before they're ready because this is reckoned to be good for their development. Boys then respond by repressing altogether their need for the tenderness which has been denied them, believing it to be either dangerously unmanly or, because they're now so unused to it, believing it must be leading straight to sex. So, of necessity, tenderness and sex have to become separated. I don't think an awful lot has changed since 1935. Tenderness is hard for many young people to accept or express because it exists somewhere between the privacy of sex and the more public gestures of friendship such as handshaking. It's intimate without necessarily being private.

Many boys regard sex *as* intimacy: a proof of love pursued urgently and sometimes with as much spite as tenderness. The intimacy of companionship, of everyday living, of a *gradually* shared privacy comes later or not at all.

I remember working in the youth centre, late one Friday night, long after the bands had packed up their equipment and the audience had gone home. I was alone in the office, counting money, when a boy I knew came in. Far from wanting to discuss the success or otherwise of the evening, he seemed distracted.

'I need to ask you something,' he said. 'Do condoms ever have holes?'

I said it was most unlikely. He said his elder brother had told him they often did. I asked why he needed to know.

'Well,' he went on, 'I've just been down the playing fields with Naomi, you know, giving her one, and I'm a bit worried.'

From his cupped hand he produced his freshly filled condom for my inspection.

'I'm going to put it in water and see if bubbles come out, like a bike tyre. Then I'll know whether it could have a hole.'

I spluttered ... but I was being trusted. I regained my composure and tried to explain that showing your used condoms to people wasn't, well, polite and that it wouldn't be such a good idea to show it to other people as this was private between himself and Naomi. He nodded agreement, quietly proud nonetheless.

Whereas boys often deal with the anxiety of intimacy by *publicising* their experience in this way or by bragging about it, many girls *privatise* that anxiety or deal with it obliquely.

Three fourteen-year-old girls visit me for a counselling appointment, worried about their friend who's going out with an older boy who 'everyone knows' has raped someone. They don't want the same thing to happen to their friend, they say, so they've tried and tried to stop her going out with him but it's useless.

I ask how they'd handle it if they really loved somebody who everyone else thought was bad. They think for a moment, then go back to talking about their friend and how stupid she's being. I ask about rape in marriage: 'If your husband raped you in the bedroom, would you divorce him?' One girl quickly says yes and they talk about their friend again. I ask how it would be if the person they loved hit them. They say they wouldn't love anyone like that in the first place, but what about their friend and the rapist? I ask how they'd handle it if the person they loved turned out to be not quite as good as they'd imagined? One of them starts talking about how she'd feel. Briefly the others join in but after two minutes they return to their friend. She's become the focus for all their current anxieties about men and sex and boundaries. How'll we be able to choose what we do and what we don't do? What'll we do if people turn out to be not as we thought?

If it's hard for young people to manage these anxieties, it's hard for parents as well. At the young people's counselling and information service where I worked, we were phoned regularly by parents, anxious about their child's uncommunicativeness. The child, by now at least thirteen or fourteen years old, would usually have become sullen and abrupt, locking the bathroom, locking the bedroom, staying out a lot, then returning 'Fine!' and 'All right!' But where from? 'Around!' and 'Why-d'you-need-to-know?' are the usual answers. While it's important never to underestimate the anxiety of parents or become complacent in assuming that young people always know what they're doing, nevertheless it seems that such secrecy is a good way for young people to practise independence. Not telling is a powerful way of staying in control, for while growing up can't be controlled, information about it certainly can be.

Some families claim to tell each other everything and parents are often nostalgic for what they remember as the golden age when 'She could tell us anything!' But the same daughters and sons remember only interrogation at breakfast, interrogation at tea. Alison was brought for counselling by her mother, and she assured the counsellor that, yes, she was happy to come and talk. But after a couple of sessions nothing in particular seemed to be the matter. Alison and the counsellor agreed to finish, where-upon, a day later, Alison's mother phoned in great indignation. Alison still wasn't talking to them at home, she reported. Not like she used to. Something *had* to be the matter because 'We've always been such a close family!' The counsellor gently suggested that perhaps it would be understandable if members of the family sometimes needed to be on their own and private, keeping certain things to themselves. Alison's behaviour need not be a rejection of her family but just a way of becoming a separate individual within it.

Not all young people need to become secretive. Most are simply ambivalent about telling parents things that matter. Some parents don't always appreciate or respect the confidentiality of what they've been told, and that's often when young people resolve to say nothing at all. But equally, I've rarely been told by a young person anything about their diary without also being told that 'My Mum went into my bedroom and read my diary!', so either mothers are pathologically nosy or diaries are not left quite as well hidden as their owners claim.

Growing up involves learning to manage the privacy of things like diaries and learning to make choices about who and how much to tell. It involves an expanding repertoire of potential confidantes. Sometimes this isn't a case of becoming dishonest with parents but rather a case of increased sensitivity.

Natalie's mother has accused her of smoking. Natalie says she doesn't want to tell her Mum that she has indeed started smoking because, apart from being scared, she doesn't want to upset her Mum, who's just lost her job. Also, she wouldn't want her Mum to tell her Dad because then he'd say she wasn't being brought up properly and would hate Natalie's Step-dad even more. 'Anyway,' Natalie says, 'I've found out things about my Mum she hasn't told me and there's probably loads of stuff about my Dad I don't know!' Her parents' secrecy may also have arisen from sensitivity rather than defensiveness. Natalie has the right to ask and her parents have the right to say nothing. From that, she'll have to draw her own conclusions.

Just as a group will pick up uncannily on its leader's own unresolved feelings, so young people like Natalie usually challenge parents at their most vulnerable. I remember a mother, managing entirely on her own, who was outraged at the company her daughter had started keeping, hanging out with much older boys. She was unable to do anything about it and petrified of what could happen to her daughter. It emerged that whenever her daughter had asked about the circumstances of her conception, fourteen years earlier, and who her father was, her mother had never been able to tell. 'She doesn't need to know! It's not important!' she insisted to me.

Pincus and Dare (1978) write that secrets and myths in families 'are always about power and dependence, about love and hate, about the wish to take care of and the wish to hurt, feelings which are inevitably bound up with sex, birth and death' (p.16). Family secrets and family myths often deal with these powerful feelings by disguising them. A counsellor's job might well be to support a young person in challenging the prevailing family culture but many young people will do that for themselves anyway, with or without anyone's support. And, in a sense, they'll do it *on behalf of* the family, because until they do, the family remains stuck in a culture which may have served it well five, ten or twenty years ago but which hasn't been able to change as the individuals in the family have changed.

Like worried parents, institutions also worry about *absolute* secrecy versus *absolute* openness. When a school thinks about employing a counsellor to attend to some of the underlying needs of students, certain anxieties immediately surface. What about parents? How will they react if they discover their child is seeing the new counsellor? What about a referral system? How will tutors keep track of students seeing this counsellor? What about confidentiality? How will teachers ever know what's going on?

These anxieties are inevitable because they're anxieties about what kinds of intimacy and privacy people can *ever* have with one another. Will a counsellor's relationship with students spoil a tutor's relationship, or will it just be a different kind of relationship? Will it spoil things for parents, or will the counsellor's relationship perhaps be more like a grandparent's? The appointment raises anxieties otherwise suppressed in daily school life. For how much does one teacher's 'open' relationship with students threaten the guardedness of another's? What happens when a student confides in the friendly receptionist rather than in his tutor? How much does the headteacher get told about individual teachers? And who's doing the telling?

Part of what makes privacy difficult in schools is that effective work can only be done through relationships and relationships involve give and take. Teachers are forever faced with dilemmas about how much of themselves to reveal. Students won't engage personally with a subject unless the teacher also does so, but how personal can a teacher afford to be? Young people will be just as scornful of total disclosure ('I myself had an abortion only a few weeks ago') as of no disclosure at all ('Never mind what I think, you just do the work!'), and particularly scornful of mixed messages: teachers open and friendly one minute, distant and authoritarian the next.

What goes on in the privacy of the staffroom is discussed by students in the same way as children might wonder what goes on in the parental bed. Which teachers fancy each other? Which don't get on? Students want to know and don't want to know. Most teachers take their cue from the headteacher as the modelling parent, whom they will typically describe as either 'formal' or 'informal', 'quite formal' or 'quite informal'. I think this is just another way of describing how the headteacher manages privacy.

The issue challenges a school at its most vulnerable because however good a school may be at applying collective rules, most schools are less good at respecting the rights of individuals. One large group is much easier to think about and manage than thirty clamouring individuals. So individuals are routinely told off in front of the whole class: something which would never happen in the staffroom. Teachers interrupt private conversations as by right, always in the name of urgency, while students' lives are often discussed in the staffroom and reported back to them: 'I didn't know your Dad had lost his job' ... 'I was sorry to hear about your sister' ... 'Fancy you needing glasses!'

Older students choose to work as student counsellors because they're aware of individuals and want to be of help, so when someone younger says, 'If I tell you something you'll keep it a secret, won't you?', it's tempting immediately to say yes. They're trained instead to resist that impulse and never offer blanket confidentiality. When someone else, full of innocent curiosity, asks them, 'Have you ever had sex?' or 'Have you ever taken drugs?', they don't answer. They know the pitfalls of answering yes; but also that, far from being dishonest or unfriendly, they can model for younger students a way of managing privacy. 'That's my business,' they might say, 'I'm not asking you about things you don't want to talk about and I'm not going to tell you things which are private to me. But just because we both keep some things private doesn't mean we can't be friends.'

Because what we use them for is so intimate, school toilets often serve as another battleground for issues of privacy. By the end of the day the signs of battle are unmistakable: toilet paper strewn, graffiti, a broken lock, fag ends. Some schools therefore provide minimalist toilets – that is, they have working taps, cubicle doors, toilet paper and seats only at the start of the week, or if you're lucky. I taught in a school where the toilets were sometimes locked altogether as a punishment. Staff, meanwhile, have their own toilets so avoid joining in this battle and influencing it in a positive way. I sometimes wonder whether inspectors or prospective parents should begin any tour of a school with a tour of its toilets and changing rooms, and should take what they find there as a sure indicator both of how the school regards its students and vice versa. One imaginative youth centre I know has an area in its girls' toilets with sofas and magazines. Other youth centres paint toilets brightly and use them to display information. These seem more helpful ways of encouraging young people to move on from experiencing a toilet as essentially someone else's *secret*, which must be exposed, to the idea of a toilet as someone else's *privacy* which can be tolerated without endangering one's own.

Privacy is no more of an issue in schools than it is in most organisations. Indeed the looser the organisation, the more likely I think it is that privacy and confidentiality won't be respected. Wherever people long to feel part of a more closely knit organisation, they trade secrets and break confidences as a way of getting closer, setting up sudden intimacies, however promiscuous or short-term they may be.

The relationship between a young person and a counsellor can be one way of exploring intimacy and privacy. Young people come to my counselling room for a first appointment excited and scared. I explain who I am. I show them the room and explain how it came to exist. I point out the phone and explain that, although unlikely, it may ring. I explain a bit about what counselling is and what it isn't, how long we'll meet for and what will happen at the end of our session. I describe the confidentiality I can offer.

Most of what I'm saying goes in one ear and out the other. The young person sits there, looking round nervously, wondering how on earth to begin. But the sense of what I'm saying is designed to *normalise* the situation. Two people are meeting to talk. It'll be private, but not a secret. It won't be weird. It might be helpful.

Anna says very little, weeping and looking away. Her silence seems to protect her. She's not even speaking to her Dad, she says. I listen and resolve to go very slowly, trusting that Anna will say more when she's ready. I might be like a Dad who *can* respect her privacy ...

Leilah describes becoming too close to her depressed Mum, becoming too much of a confidante ...

Stewart talks about his frantic one-night stands and his drug use, none of which give him the closeness he's always craved from his Dad ...

Kate describes how sexual abuse in the family has made it really hard to trust people ...

Glen talks about his relationship with Alanah. They've been going out together since she was thirteen and he was fourteen. He really loves her, he says, but thinks maybe they should split up now, before he goes to university. She's been talking about feeling stale. I ask whether he wants them to split up. He says he's not sure. He doesn't want Alanah to feel trapped ...

Nathan regales me with tales of drinking and fighting and crying with mates and how it's still never enough. He doesn't arrive for his next appointment ...

Shan describes feeling exploited by other people. Then, 'That's enough of me!' she says. 'Now I want to know all about you!'

Ellie describes how much more satisfying the cuddling is afterwards than the sex ...

And despite my invitations, Lewis still can't say goodbye. He phones the day after our last session and leaves a message on the answerphone, thanking me and saying the goodbye that he can manage.

These are all stories about intimacy. Talking, we make sense of some things. Other things still don't make sense but feel better for having been talked about. But running through all these stories and as important as making sense of anything is the relationship between the young person and the counsellor. Will that relationship be too close or too distant? Will it be shared or will one person dominate? Will the counsellor know when to persist and when to back off? Stage-managed though it may be, this relationship is just as real as any other, and for the young person it's the chance to test again the boundaries of intimacy and privacy, seeing what feels comfortable and what doesn't. It's the chance to discover something *mutually* respectful, for without confidence in these limits, we deceive and hurt one another. Without a sense of where our own boundaries are and the confidence to insist on them, we allow others to hurt us. Without understanding and sensing other people's boundaries, we do the same to them.

CHAPTER 10

See You Around
How Schools Manage Endings

It was the end of the summer term at the end of another school year. At the school where I worked as the counsellor, we were saying goodbye to four teachers leaving for other teaching jobs, to one teacher leaving to start a different career, to another who'd decided not to return from maternity leave, another taking a year off to write, to two others moving with their families to Cambodia and France, and to two whose short-term contracts had run out. All this, when earlier in the term we'd already said goodbye to 139 Year 11 students (fifteen to sixteen-year-olds), 14 Year 12 students (sixteen to seventeen-year-olds) and 49 Year 13 students. As usual the staffroom was full of mixed feelings: regret and relief, embarrassment and glee. It was, after all, the end of everyone's year and the beginning of a proper holiday.

Endings matter. Unless we say goodbye, unless we separate properly, we struggle to begin the next phase of our lives and are left hankering instead after old securities – the way a few students who've left school always seem to be wandering round the site, trying to work out what's happened, or the way some teachers who've retired hurry back immediately to do supply work.

Schools are beset with endings: people and plans move ahead throughout the year, frantic to get to the next stage, the next module, topic, chapter, anxious never to be left behind. Endings are therefore happening all the time, yet come to seem like a perpetual administrative nuisance in schools rather than a series of important developmental opportunities.

On the other hand, schools are experts at beginnings. So much is at stake. If things get off to a bad start every teacher and every student knows how hard it is to recover. Teachers return to school early in September. First lessons are meticulously prepared. Students are then allowed to return in stages. Settling-in time is anticipated and allowed for. And all this planning has actually begun the previous January at senior management meetings: sorting out the budget, sorting out staffing, sorting out the new timetable, rising to a crescendo of planning involving almost everybody by the end of the summer term: all to make sure everything is ready for the beginning.

We have much less invested in endings. Endings are difficult. By the end of the year the teacher and class are tired and have decidedly mixed feelings about each other. When almost every school relationship has inevitably been a mixed experience, it's difficult to know how to acknowledge that. So teachers and students tend to categorise one another as good or bad. Rarely both. At the end of the day neither party has entirely lived up to the other's expectations, so it's just easier to dismiss one another and think, in effect, good riddance.

Teachers rarely get affirmation for themselves from anybody, so they find it hard to give that affirmation to students with whom they've rowed, chased deadlines, cajoled and by whom they've sometimes felt bullied. Report-writing can be one way of taking revenge. After all, the students can always start again: they can grow up, move on, make fresh relationships with other people, but the teachers never get to talk about what all this feels like or about the fact of saying goodbye every year to so many students for whom they actually cared. They don't get to say how *wearing* it feels always to be letting go. Or what a relief!

I remember when the time came as a classroom teacher to tell my A-level class that I would be having a term's secondment away from school during the summer term of their final exams. I was fed up and exhausted with teaching, though I cared a lot about this class. I felt a mixture of extreme guilt and extreme relief to think I wouldn't be teaching them for the final weeks of their course. I told them the news in as matter-of-fact a way as possible, disguising my horribly mixed feelings. I told them they were fine students so it wouldn't matter in the slightest who taught them. One student, whom I'd taught for five years, asked a couple of factual questions, then burst into tears and ran out. I felt angry with her, thinking (and saying) how unprofessional she was, all the while completely unable to acknowledge my own sadness or my guilty feeling of abandoning her and refusing absolutely to acknowledge my role in her life as someone upon whom she depended, not just academically, but also for some degree of self-worth. Her father had left home when she was nine: now here was I, her long-time teacher, leaving her at what must have felt like a crucial time in her life, apparently without a care.

I wish I'd handled the situation differently, with more compassion and wisdom. I wish someone had explained to me what transference is, how powerfully it can be present in student–teacher relationships, and how to cope with this student's transference of feelings about her father on to me as her teacher. I wish someone had helped me think about how it felt to be leaving this class and how odd it was to be temporarily leaving the school.

Every week, every year in school we attempt to sustain and develop as many as three hundred human relationships. We accept that our work is a personal business and that we're only as effective as the relationships we manage to make with each other and with our students, yet we allow ourselves no time to reflect upon our part in those relationships and the effect they have on us. We do enjoy varying degrees of managerial supervision, appraisal and review, concentrating on the professional parts of ourselves, but these processes are always affected by the fact that our managers will be writing our references and in many ways determining our professional futures.

Staff need an opportunity regularly to review and reflect upon working relationships, individual circumstances and specific pieces of work; an opportunity to develop as individuals within our professional roles by addressing the personal as well as the professional in what we do; an opportunity to become clearer about our feelings, ideas, reactions, choices in order to move on. Such a reviewing process is best done with someone from outside the institution. There's nothing to stop a school setting up such a facility for itself, with a choice of appropriately qualified people advertised in the staffroom and with staff free to meet with these people in complete confidentiality, the school simply being invoiced at the end of the sessions. At the very least this is an extremely cost-effective facility, with thousands of pounds potentially saved on cover for staff who will otherwise deal with stress, isolation or confusion by not coming to school at all. It is, furthermore, one way of helping us manage those times in our lives when things are changing or ending.

Form tutors aim to be just such a facility for their students, yet in practice students only get to talk to their form tutors with twenty-nine other people around, or on their own only if there's been a crisis. In most schools there's no built-in mechanism for talking regularly, privately, as a matter of course. When they're about to leave, students may at the very least need a final individual tutorial as one way of ending: a chance methodically to retrace their time in school and anticipate the future, about which they're bound to have mixed feelings. A twelve-year-old girl told me recently, 'My Dad wants me to be big but he doesn't want me to grow up.' I think she was telling me about her own ambivalence about growing up as well as her Dad's.

Bowlby (1979) developed various ideas about attachment and separation from observing the behaviour of babies in hospital, separated from their mothers. He noticed three stages of a baby's response to this situation: first protest, then despair

and then detachment or denial, each of which he likened to processes of mourning following any bereavement, processes
which might happen regardless of a person's age. He noted,
though, that the older the *child*, the more likely it is that
detachment and denial will occur prematurely as that child's
way of dealing with its conflicting anger towards and yearning
for the lost person. In schools it's easy to see this happening. The
lost person could, in effect, be a significant teacher, a form tutor,
or the school itself. So every time a student claims, 'When I've
left I'm never coming back! This school totally stinks!', it's interesting to wonder whether another equally vehement feeling is
being denied: 'I'm really scared about leaving school. What'll
become of me?'

In some schools a particularly manic behaviour has become
traditional among Year 11 students whereby on their last official
day in school they frantically sign and draw on each other's
school shirts with felt pens: this, in addition to other traditional
behaviours like getting drunk and playing practical jokes. Here,
feelings of grief are avoided by being turned desperately into
celebration, with no place for mixed feelings. Yet signing one
another's shirts seems to be at the same time an expression of
great intimacy – a way of touching and of saying affectionate
things to one another – as well as an expression of anger: the
shirts are essentially being vandalised. A few students, walking
out of school at the end of the last day, will also look to vandalise
something quickly (a dustbin, a display, a noticeboard), as much
as to say, 'I hate you!', but will at the same time look to take away
a souvenir as much as to say, 'I love you!' These apparently contradictory impulses are evident in other situations where separation occurs. Bowlby's idea is that the way a child deals with
such confusion, loving and hating the lost person or, in this case,
lost institution, is by denying *both* feelings, and that this denial is
unhealthy in the long run.

Within the bounds of what school rules can cope with I think
it's important to allow these feelings and acknowledge that

they're real, not silly. In some schools mentoring schemes exist whereby students can talk regularly on their own with a trusted teacher, reviewing progress and taking stock. This is important for students to be able to do, and particularly in periods of transition. We all need opportunities to look back, to think about what our experience has been like, what's been helpful and what hasn't. In this way we allow ourselves potentially to express both our love and our hate, our satisfactions and our disappointments. Teachers need to do this when they leave jobs just as much as their students do when they leave school. The few students who leave mid-year need it too because they often get little help. Their friends either abandon them prematurely or cling on for dear life. 'Are you looking forward to your new school?' must be an impossible question to answer.

Departing school students act out the same behaviours as a young person leaving a counselling relationship, who will either say, 'I'm feeling brilliant! I can't wait to leave!' suggesting 'I never needed you anyway!', or something like 'I'll probably see you around!' suggesting 'I'm not *really* leaving, am I?' Sometimes the counsellor gets punished for his or her apparent neglect in *allowing* the person to leave: young people start coming late or not coming at all, rejecting the counsellor in order not to feel rejected. So counsellors resolutely encourage young people to talk about the approaching end of the relationship: what it's been like, what it's meant, what's been helpful and what hasn't.

As in formally therapeutic relationships, many Year 11 students appear to regress briefly before leaving school. Where a person in counselling will revive his or her original symptoms ('I'm still no better than I was when I started!'), Year 11 students will seem especially chaotic and demanding, just like the Year 7 students they once were. We accuse them of 'seeking attention' as if that were a heinous crime rather than a natural response to possibly the most significant separation they've experienced since babyhood. We accuse them of being 'immature' and threaten them with the outside world which, of course, is precisely what they're trying to avoid. Because we habitually praise independence in school, the expression of continuing attachment is regarded as almost shameful, so students express detachment and independence as ostentatiously as possible: 'I can't wait to leave!'

The school student like the child, like the baby, clings, in part, to the institutional breast and rails against its withdrawal. But this attached student also, in part, genuinely does look forward to leaving school and feels guilty about abandoning the breast ('Who will my teachers have now I'm gone?'), so makes a defensive psychological adjustment so as to experience the school as actually rejecting *him or her* in order not to feel so personally responsible ('Yeah, teachers have always hated me!').

One of the problems for departing Year 11 and Year 13 students is that their endings are necessarily so staggered. Year 11 officially leave mid-way through May but will all be coming back to school later in the month, possibly for revision lessons and certainly for exams. Many of them will then return for Year 12 induction in July and return all over again in September to start another two years of school. Equally, Year 13 will officially leave school in May, will return throughout June for exams, may then have official leaving parties after the exams and will probably return again in mid-August to collect their exam results and in some cases, with the school's help, negotiate university entrance. All this means it's hard for students to make much sense of an actual ending anyway. If anyone was looking to avoid the painful reality of ending, then this structure encourages them. It does mean, though, that there is even more need for the school to establish and mark its own clear, final ending. *When* this ending happens matters less than the fact that it *is* marked and *how* it's marked.

Assemblies can be important opportunities to mark endings and beginnings, but I was struck in one end-of-year assembly by how tempting it is to find something comfortingly tangible to base a final assembly around, in this case a whole series of sporting awards: trophies and certificates handed out to great applause. Records of achievement also sometimes get handed out in this way.

But it's much harder to mark our intangible achievements, the many other ways in which we've moved on as people. One of the best final school assemblies I've witnessed was devised, not by senior teachers, but by the RE department. In many ways it was like a memorial service, with readings, dimmed lighting, some time for silent reflection and some music. The students, not the staff, contributed the readings and played the music, not all of the pieces solemn – some funny, some irreverent. It seemed as if we were honouring the many different aspects of our shared experience as a school, both mourning and celebrating the end of the year. People left the assembly hall looking thoughtful and calm.

In many cultures the transition from child to adult is marked with accompanying ritual. Nelson Mandela (1994) has written about how at the age of sixteen ritual circumcision marked his incorporation into the adult society of his tribe. In British culture it used to be the case that a person's twenty-first birthday marked that transition. More recently eighteenth birthdays have become significant, with families trying to find appropriate ways of marking the beginning of their child's legal adulthood. But there are plenty of unofficial transitions (driving tests, sexual experiences, jobs), and it's become harder to know what to mark. In the absence of any consensus, public examinations have become the milestone.

We do everything we can to prepare students for these exams. We fill them with knowledge, with techniques. Desperately we teach them revision skills, even though by Year 11 they've already taken plenty of internal school exams in their lives. But however hard we try, we can't minimise the importance of these particular exams and so students inevitably seek to avoid them, whether in idleness, denying their anxiety, or in desperate cramming, trying to conquer the anxiety of not knowing, not having the answer. For however frantic the talking, the revision, the good luck messages beforehand, students enter and sit down in a large, silent room always finally alone, equal, unable to communicate any further, facing the prepared-for but ultimately unknown questions.

We think of exams as about school, but they're about far more than that: they're about growing up, moving on, anticipating our own eventual end. In a way exams prepare us, not for life, but for death. The big clock ticks inexorably. The birds sing outside. Exams are finally, inescapably *there*, and inside the large hall we're all faced with the same dilemma: whether to abandon ourselves to the essential meaninglessness of it all and write nothing or whether to try hard and invest in the thought of an afterlife: the consolation of good results. After exams life goes on but is never the same. We're defined in terms of our results: how we did. How we di(e)d.

In supporting students both before and during exams I think it's helpful to think about our needs in relation to death and dying. Such needs are considerable, difficult, hard to talk about, and as carers we rarely get it right. There is, of course, a difference between dying and graduating, between the finality of death and the *transition* that is graduation or exams. But the same question lurks beneath both experiences: what's all this for?

A small child will ask, 'Why do people die?', while a teenager will no longer ask that question directly but is always implicitly asking a version of the same question, 'Why do I have to grow up?', or explicitly, 'Why do I have to do this?' School students do have experience in their lives of important people and animals dying, but that isn't an experience we usually dwell on in school. We call it 'morbid', because schools suffer from the same cultural paralysis about death as the rest of society. Students tell me in counselling about not being allowed to go to funerals and how cheated they're left feeling. Parents think they're being kind, protecting their child from pain, but the child always reports that, yes, of course I'd have been upset but I'd still rather have been there.

When a friend's mother or father dies, students are both fascinated and appalled. They don't know whether to ask questions and talk about it or to keep a respectful distance. They look to teachers to give the lead. But teachers, in turn, are often caught up in the same dilemma, perhaps reminded of their own bereavements when, again, they didn't know what to do because, again, no one showed them how. In one school I know, during the week after a student died and as the school was struggling to come to terms with the loss, no less than five boys were suspended for various incidents of fighting. Until then, no one had been suspended all year. Fighting seemed to be the only way the boys knew.

Leaving school is a chance to learn a little about dying. There are symbolic stories from around the world dealing with transition and with dying (Gersie 1991) which are useful in helping us think about and recognise our own experience from the distance a story affords. But we also need to tell our own stories. The groups I run in schools have short lifetimes but it's always important to end them properly. Students usually try to avoid any sort of ending. At the last session someone will always ask, 'Can't we carry on after today?'

I usually take time to think with the group about what's been useful about our work together *and* what hasn't, to tell one another what's been valuable about each other's contribution. I use a final exercise where I tell the group to wander around the room in silence. I tell them to stop, all together. Then wander again. Then stop. I explain that they're now to continue wandering and stopping all together in their own time, in silence, without any instruction from me but simply by being aware of each other's movement. They do this easily for a few minutes and the group ends there with them in control, working together. They're always amazed that they've managed this and leave, delighted with themselves.

There are many ways of ending. What matters is that we do, somehow, end. As another summer term draws to a close, one team of Year 13 student counsellors I supervise has been wrestling with the end of their year's work. They've had a good year, working supportively with lots of younger students in school, and they're leaving to be replaced by a new team. I've been emphasising to them the importance of ending properly with the younger students they know. I've told them to start saying goodbye early, don't leave it until the last minute; whatever you do, say something; try to bring up the fact of your leaving in every conversation; if you don't say goodbye properly, it'll make life much harder for next year's team because people will still be attached to you and it's not fair to keep them hanging on after you've left; remember that some of the people you've got to know this year have experienced divorce and were *not* told what was happening because their parents were scared and thought it was kinder that way; don't be surprised if some people tell you they don't care whether you leave or not; don't be surprised if others become tearful and panicky. Let them feel their feelings, let them talk about it.

Just like beginnings, endings need thinking about and planning. It's hard to end properly, but it matters.

References

Bannister, A. (1995) 'Dramatherapy and Psychodrama with children.' *British Journal of Psychodrama and Sociodrama 10, 2.*

Becker, E. (1973) *The Denial of Death.* New York: Free Press.

Behr, H. (1988) 'Group analysis with early adolescents.' *Group Analysis 21.*

Bion, W.R. (1961) *Experiences in Groups.* London: Routledge.

Bond, E. (1973) *The Sea.* London: Eyre Methuen.

Bowlby, J. (1973) *Separation, Anger and Anxiety.* London: Hogarth Press.

Bowlby, J. (1979) *The Making and Breaking of Affectional Bonds.* London: Routledge.

Camus, A. (1942) *L'Etranger.* London: Penguin Books.

Cupitt, D. (1984) *The Sea of Faith.* London: BBC Books.

Daniel, S., Jacks, J., Misiorowski, B. and Vajna, A. (1993) *Tombstone.* USA: Panavion/Cinergi.

Denny, S. (1973) *What Is True?* London: Jardinière Music.

Doors, The. (1967) *People Are Strange.* USA: Doors Music Co.

Emunah, R. (1995) 'From adolescent trauma to adolescent drama.' In S. Jennings (ed) *Dramatherapy with Children and Adolescents.* London: Routledge.

Enfield, H. (1997) *Harry Enfield and Chums.* London: BBC Worldwide Ltd.

Evans, J. (1998) *Active Analytic Group Therapy for Adolescents.* London: Jessica Kingsley Publishers.

Fiedler, L. (1960) *Love and Death in the American Novel.* New York: Criterion.

Foulkes, S.H. (1975) *Group Analytic Psychotherapy.* London: Gordon & Breach.

Freud, S. (1900) *The Interpretation of Dreams.* London: Penguin Books.

Freud, S. (1905) *Jokes and Their Relation to the Unconscious.* London: Penguin Books.

Gersie, A. (1991) *Storymaking in Bereavement.* London: Jessica Kingsley Publishers.

Golding, W. (1954) *Lord of the Flies.* London: Faber.

Hagelthorn, C. (1990) 'War and peace: on psychodramatic role theory.' *British Journal of Psychodrama and Sociodrama 5*, 1.

Holmes, P. (1992) *The Inner World Outside*. London: Routledge.

Hornby, N. (1992) *Fever Pitch*. London: Victor Gollancz.

Hornby, N. (1995) *High Fidelity*. London: Victor Gollancz.

Housman, A.E. (1956) 'Last poems xii.' In *Collected Poems*. London: Penguin Books.

Hughes, T. (1979) 'Ravens.' In *Moortown*. London: Faber.

Irvin, J. (1998) 'The angel of Avalon.' In *Mojo Magazine*. London: EMAP Metro.

Keats, J. (1817) 'Letter to George and Tom Keats.' In R. Gittings (ed) *Letters*. Oxford: Oxford University Press.

Klein, M. (1932) *The Psycho-analysis of Children*. London: Hogarth Press.

Kristeva, J. (1991) *Strangers to Ourselves*. New York: Columbia University Press.

Lewis, J.P. (1992) 'New baby.' In J. Foster (ed) *Another Very First Poetry Book*. Oxford: Oxford University Press.

Mandela, N. (1994) *Long Walk to Freedom*. London: Little, Brown & Co.

Meltzer, D. (1973) *Sexual States of Mind*. Scotland: Clunie Press.

Menzies Lyth, I. (1988) *Containing Anxiety in Institutions*. London: Free Association Books.

Mitchell, J. (1971) *All I Want*. USA: Joni Mitchell Music.

Moreno, J.L. (1961) 'The role concept, a bridge between psychiatry and sociology.' In J. Fox (ed) *The Essential Moreno*. New York: Springer.

Moreno, J.L. (1972) *Psychodrama Volume 1*. New York: Beacon House.

Morrison, B. (1997) *As If*. London: Granta Books.

Nietzsche, F. (1968) *Twilight of the Idols*. Translated by R.J. Holingdale. London: Penguin Books.

Phillips, A. (1993) *On Kissing, Tickling and Being Bored*. London: Faber.

Phillips, A. (1995) *Terrors and Experts*. London: Faber.

Pincus, L and Dare, C. (1978) *Secrets in the Family*. London: Faber.

Pitzele, P. (1991) 'Adolescents inside out.' In P. Holmes and M. Karp (eds) *Psychodrama: Inspiration and Technique*. London: Routledge.

Sayers, J. (1998) *Boy Crazy*. London: Routledge.

Supergrass (1995). *Alright*. London: EMI Records.

Suttie, I. (1935) *The Origins of Love and Hate*. London: Kegan Paul.

Thompson, H. (1997) *Peter Cook: A Biography*. UK: Hodder & Stoughton.

Winnicott, D.W. (1964) *The Child, the Family and the Outside World*. London: Penguin Books.

Winnicott, D.W. (1965) *The Maturational Processes and the Facilitating Environment*. London: Karnac Books.

Winnicott, D.W. (1971) *Playing and Reality*. London: Routledge.

Subject Index

Author Index